READING AND DISCRIMINATION

DENYS THOMPSON

STEPHEN TUNNICLIFFE

READING

AND

DISCRIMINATION

New Edition, completely rewritten

1979

CHATTO & WINDUS

LONDON

Published by
Chatto & Windus Ltd
London

*

Clarke, Irwin & Co. Ltd
Toronto

First published 1934
Reprinted 1936, 1939, 1942, 1947, 1949, 1951
Revised and reprinted 1954, 1955,
1957, 1959, 1962, 1963, 1965 1973
This new and completely rewritten edition 1979

British Library Cataloguing in Publication Data

Thompson, Denys
Reading and discrimination.—New ed.
1. Criticism
I. Title   II. Tunnicliffe, Stephen
801'.95   PN83

ISBN 0–7011–2359–1
ISBN 0–7011–2360–5   Pbk.

CONTENTS

FOREWORD

The continuing demand for a book originally planned to meet conditions very different from those of today is an indication that its general approach to the close study of literature is still valid. Although little of the first edition (1934) has survived our almost total re-writing, the aim and general structure remain the same. The book we now offer, the outcome of word-for-word collaboration, provides a course in close reading with a wide selection of passages for practice.

The forty or so years during which the original book has been in circulation have seen great changes in English literature; we have recorded the most significant of these in the text, and our anthology takes account of them. In particular, we have decided to include a number of dramatic excerpts, more examples of literature from overseas, and a higher proportion of contemporary examples. Some of the authors now represented were not born when the first edition appeared.

Our debt to other writers and critics will be apparent. It would be impossible to name them all and invidious to select a few. In any case, we hope our readers will be encouraged to turn first to the complete works and authors we have sampled rather than to other anthologies or books of criticism, however perspicacious. Finally, we wish to record our gratitude to Hilary Tunnicliffe and Jim Preston for practical assistance with chapters one to three, and to Marion Maynard for converting a heap of miscellaneous books and papers into a neat and accurate typescript.

Denys Thompson, Stephen Tunnicliffe

PART ONE

LANGUAGE AND LITERATURE

CHAPTER I

LANGUAGE

Where language starts

Man is distinguished from other living creatures by his power of speech, for no animal has the physical or mental equipment to produce it. Animals can make sounds to keep in touch while hunting, like owls or timber wolves; they can show feelings, such as excitement, anger and frustration; they can make calls to further the pursuit of biological ends, such as mating. But that is all. Moreover, the ability to speak is not just one of a number of characteristics that put mankind into a particular classificatory slot. It is a faculty at the core of his very being, the means of all the advances he can make as an individual or as a member of a group. The young child, for example, starts to familiarise himself with his world first by means of touch; next he associates words with things and actions; finally by the time he reaches adulthood he no longer needs to explore by getting hold of things, for he has learned to replace physical exploration by the use of symbols, in particular language.

Given the chance to manipulate speech, to see how it works, and to note its almost magical effects, a child will learn his language in spite of appalling handicaps, such as congenital blindness or deafness or gross parental neglect. In fact language is so deeply rooted, so inextricably involved in every human thought and so many human activities, that it is difficult to suppress. The skills needed to develop language are innate, as universal in mankind as walking upright. The equipment for producing grammatical speech is built into every healthy human being. 'Universal grammar is of a unique type, common to all men, and it is entirely the by-product of peculiar modes of cognition based upon the biological constitution of the individual.' Thus a child's language is not just a mirroring of what he hears, not just part of a cultural tradition handed on from generation to generation. The individual is not merely a vessel to be filled, but an independent unit. His speech is set going by social contact, but it will continue working only if the child re-creates the whole language mechanism out of the raw material available to him. He makes up language by himself.

It is easy to speculate about the origin of language because no one can be proved wrong. At present a well-argued view is that the first language developed from the rhythmic noises made by early men as they danced round a fire or cult-object, and that the first units of speech were short sentences rather than separate words. This primitive singing brought its users closer to each other, conveying emotions and states of feeling rather than facts or instructions; it was poetry rather than prose. The practical uses of language may have come later, as human consciousness developed; we may imagine it as providing means of contact among the members of a family foraging for food in a forest, or for transmitting calls of warning against falling rocks or rising floods. Biologically then language evolved as part of a survival mechanism, so that today the sounds of the human voice come to us after many thousands of years of experience; they reach back to our very earliest days when we were just beginning to be human.

Language and the individual

Thus a deep-rooted language is central in a child's growth; he learns it as he becomes more conscious of himself and his surroundings. He finds that words can be substituted for physical acts and begins to use them in contexts other than those in which they were learned. Language not only helps a child to perceive more discriminately – 'You see much more of the wood when you know the names of the trees' – but probably also to move more efficiently and to adjust himself physically with greater accuracy. Eventually his language will supply him with many of the guide-lines, good or less good, by which he will steer or drift his way through life. 'The child's perception of reality takes its structure and patterning from language, as his acquisition of this enables him to sort out his impressions into generalised categories incorporating the accumulated experience of past generations' (Frank Whitehead).

If you alter a child's language you alter his character. Perhaps we can best illustrate one of the ways in which words affect character, as the individual digests the content of words so that it becomes part of him, by taking as an example the word *love*. As we all know, it has depth of meaning and a wide field of reference. We love our parents perhaps; if we are fortunate we may love our work; we may, like Christ, love humanity; we are here because our parents fell in love. All of us have loved or been loved, and we know that it is not a trivial experience, the expression of mere liking or fancy or desire. When a man tells a girl he loves her, or *vice versa*, he or she may be making the profoundest statement of a life-time. The word has a powerful charge of meaning, and some of this it has gathered from its use over hundreds of years by poets, the Bible, dramatists and novelists. Of 'love' and 'beauty' Owen Barfield has this to say:

Every time we abuse these terms, or use them too lightly, we are draining them of their power; every time a society journalist or a film producer exploits this vast suggestiveness to tickle a vanity or dignify a lust, he is squandering a great pile of spiritual capital which has been laid up by centuries of weary effort.

(History in English Words)

Examples come from all the ages of English literature, starting with the Bible, from the great love cycle, the Song of Solomon, in the Old Testament to the words – which still ring memorably – of St Paul's letter to the Christians at Rome in the New Testament:

Neither death, nor life, nor angels, nor principalities, nor powers, nor things present, nor things to come, nor height, nor depth, nor any other creature, shall be able to separate us from the love of God.

Then there are proverbial expressions, like the one in Shakespeare, 'The course of true love never did run smooth', or the words of the French song: 'It's love that makes the world go round'. In the poets there are hundreds of instances; here is only one, a lyric by the Scottish poet Robert Burns:

A Red, Red Rose

O my luve is like a red, red rose,
    That's newly sprung in June:
O my luve is like the melodie,
    That's sweetly play'd in tune.

As fair art thou, my bonie lass,
    So deep in luve am I;
And I will luve thee still, my dear,
    Till a' the seas gang dry.

Till a' the seas gang dry, my dear,
    And the rocks melt wi' the sun;
And I will luve thee still, my dear,
    While the sands o' life shall run.

And fare-thee-weel, my only luve!
    And fare-thee-weel a while!
And I will come again, my luve,
    Tho' it were ten thousand mile.

Words store up riches of meaning from the contexts they are used in; and our stock of well-endowed words shapes the ideas by which we live. We manage our lives by making hundreds of little decisions influenced quite unconsciously by our notions of such things as good and evil; so that our lives are altered if the value of words like *virtue, nobility, honour, honesty* and *generosity* is weakened. In fact all these words have lost the strength they used to possess, and it is difficult now to use them naturally and convincingly. It is ideas shaped in words that sustain the climber immobilised by bad weather on a dangerous ledge, the swimmer holding up a half-drowned person, the prisoner shut up for religious or political beliefs in solitary confinement or a concentration camp, the nurse coping for hours with a difficult birth or the casualties of an air crash.

Forms of language

Language takes many forms, each with a different vocabulary, a different style, a different delivery for a particular audience. Scientific research, shouts of support from spectators, hymns in church, gossip in a pub . . . all have their special kinds of language. Even within a single type of reading matter, such as the novel, there is immense variety, from stories specially designed to kill time on a long journey or after illness (when conditions anyway don't permit much in the way of concentration) to closely written fiction, like that of D. H. Lawrence, in which every word counts towards the effect the writer is aiming at.

In our view language is at its fullest and most flexible when creative imaginations are drawing on it for drama, fiction, poetry and song. Such forms of language are infinitely rich and varied, covering the whole range of human experience. At first hearing, this claim for the supremacy of imaginative language may sound extravagant. Isn't the language of science, it may be argued, the most important of all? Science determines our idea of the universe, supplies a good deal of our knowledge of our environment, makes possible the technology by which we live the kinds of life we lead. Although most scientific investigation requires mathematics, the language of numbers, more than that of words, science's ways of employing language are certainly very important and very useful, and (as we shall notice later on) could be used to advantage beyond the boundaries of science. Language used scientifically supplies us with an intelligible mode of communication, and one that is particularly valuable for detecting and deflating the phenomenal amount of concealed propaganda, commercial and political, that infects the atmosphere and makes it difficult to think straight and act rightly. However, in our technological, machine-dominated world, we tend to admire the rational, scientific uses of language, and to neglect the language appropriate to our emotions and feelings. This narrows our humanity. If we haven't got much in the way of language for expressing and conveying what we feel we are so much the more inarticulate – 'dumb', as we say – and rather less human. There is also a tendency for the language appropriate to science and technology to encroach on areas of experience where it is inappropriate, even misleading. Take for example education, that subtle exchange between teacher and taught which forms so important a part of a person's growing up. If we talk about it in such terms as input, throughput, systems analysis, cost-accounting, feed-back, flow, results, finished products and so on, as some people do, we shall come to regard schools and colleges as factories and students as raw materials to be processed. Reduced to these technological concepts education would become dehumanised and eventually sterile.

Language at its most potent

The most characteristic form of imaginative language is poetry. It is worth recalling that both poetry and science sprang from the same source – the desire of men to understand and control their environment. For a thousand years or so poetry was the main medium for writing about science, not only because verse was easy to remember when the ability to write was rare and printing non-existent, but also because poetry was regarded as the finest means of expressing matters of the greatest importance to man. Moreover in some languages, including English, poetry from the start was a more disciplined and intelligible mode of expression than prose. A fine example of this is the *De Rerum Natura* (On the Nature of Things) by the Roman poet Lucretius, who expounded the Greek atomic theory with compelling poetic power. If you want an example, look up the opening of the poem – an impressive address to Venus, goddess of love, as the origin of all life. Lucretius's work was both the best science and the best poetry of its time. It was not until printing became easy and cheap that verse was abandoned as the vehicle for scientific knowledge, including medicine.

This unity of science and poetry need not surprise us when we consider that imagination fuels the finest forms of both. Obviously this applies to poetry, but it is also true of science. The great scientists are those who leap the gulf, to land on a brilliant hypothesis that lightens the darkness and is then proved by research to be valid. Copernicus for example found that the orbits of planets would look simpler if they were seen from the sun. His first step, then, was a leap of the imagination: to leave the earth and put himself on to the sun. Later the ground gained by Kepler and Kekulé was first opened up by the imagination; the latter thought up his theory of the benzene ring after a day-dream about snakes eating their tails. In this century Rutherford and Bohr and Einstein are familiar examples of similar imaginative powers. Moreover, as the speculations of physicists appear wilder and wilder to the layman, farther and farther beyond the power of language to express, the mind can grasp them only by means of metaphor, the key device of poetry. Attempts to explain them in the language of rational discourse have strained words beyond their capacity to carry meaning. For instance, physicists tell us about a universe that is finite, but unconfined; expanding, but expanding into nothing; and of electrons capable of passing through space without taking any time to do so.

From a biological point of view the imagination was evolved as a piece of survival mechanism. It was the group of early men who imagined that an overhanging cliff might fall on their settlement and took evasive action that survived; and one can conceive many other examples. Since then the imagination has impelled every advance, spiritual, mental or material that man has made. To suggest one illustration: the specifically human quality of altruism, unselfishness, the ability to get outside oneself and inside another human being, and think and feel as he does, has been the drive behind some of the greatest deeds of humanity. The great dramatists and novelists use the same ability when they imagine for us how different people live, and so open up fresh possibilities of living for us. Imagination is a quality that is very badly needed nowadays. To give examples at extremes: in everyday life and business all those whose words and acts may affect other people – tax officials, rate-collectors, politicians, social security officials, teachers, policemen, doctors and every driver on the road – need to visualise the concrete results for others of their policies and behaviour. On another plane, society as a whole stands in urgent want of imagination in its members to foresee the directions we are moving in and the destinations we may reach; and to see that our courses are steered, not just allowed to drift. We should keep the faculty alive by means of every form of drama, art, song, and fiction.

Telling a story

The oldest, and still the most widespread and popular form of entertainment is the telling of a story. Originally this was purely oral: the storyteller had a recognised place in society, and his skill was appreciated and rewarded. This is still true, but in our day the response to a story is often very far removed from, and perhaps out of proportion to, the skill of the storyteller. Today many such fictional representations still come to us orally but through television, film and radio, all of which impose a technological barrier between source and listener. We get from fictional stories especially strong impressions of how other human beings live, believe, think and feel, because fiction involves us at a very primitive level. The makers of some television documentaries, emulated now by practitioners of the new journalism in the U.S.A. and in this country, have recognised this in creating hybrid forms uneasily poised between fiction and fact. Nevertheless the most accessible and probably still the most popular form of fiction is the novel. A good novel offers us new experiences through our imagination. The writer believes in what he imagines through his characters; he describes their thoughts and feelings and actions, but never from a neutral point of view. Joseph Conrad put it thus:

Every subject in the region of intellect and emotion must have a morality of its own if it is treated at all sincerely; and even the most artful of writers will give himself (and his morality) away in about every third sentence.

(*Chance*)

Inevitably the novelist has his own sense of values, his own idea of what matters, what is interesting in life, what makes it worth living; and his stories cannot fail to express these ideas. Unwittingly we modify from fiction our ideas of what human beings are and how they are likely to behave, and develop our attitudes – of admiration or disapproval – of the way they conduct themselves. Thus fiction has the power of increasing or diminishing our ability to live. The novelist Storm Jameson puts it this way:

You take up a novel in the definite expectation of being pleased or entertained. In consequence your mind is prepared to receive everything the novelist is offering. You are lucky if all he offers you is a good plot. In most cases what he is offering is something much more insidious. He is offering you his attitude to life.

Other novelists have told us explicitly that they do aim to influence their readers, to extend the bounds of their experience. D. H. Lawrence for instance wrote: 'I do write because I want folk – English folk – to alter and have more sense.' And later:

Only in the novel are *all* things given full play, or at least, they may be given full play, when we realise that life itself, and not inert safety, is the reason for living. For out of the full play of all things emerges the only thing that is anything, the wholeness of a man, the wholeness of a woman, man alive, and live woman.

READING AND DISCRIMINATION

Poetry

This applies as well to poetry and drama. The writers of these offer us perceptive accounts of human behaviour because they want to say something, and they see more clearly and feel more sensitively than the rest of us. If the writing is good, it increases our awareness of other human beings, adds to our knowledge of them, develops our sympathy, and extends our insight into the way the world is going. That is a pretty inclusive claim, and only the greatest writers like Shakespeare and Tolstoy get all these results at once. Because imaginative literature involves us so fully it can often be disturbing. This short poem by William Blake, for instance, presents an unexpected, even shocking image of babyhood:

Infant Sorrow

> My mother groan'd! my father wept.
> Into the dangerous world I leapt:
> Helpless, naked, piping loud:
> Like a fiend hid in a cloud.
>
> Struggling in my father's hands,
> Striving against my swadling bands,
> Bound and weary I thought best
> To sulk upon my mother's breast.

More ordinary poets writing quite simple poems can give us the delight of recognition: 'That's just how I see it', 'Just what I feel', 'I've often thought that'. That particular pleasure was the one most highly esteemed in the eighteenth century; in Pope's words:

> True wit is nature to advantage dressed:
> What oft was thought, but ne'er so well expressed.

There is plenty of evidence that this is still an approach to poetry that both poets and readers subscribe to. Here are two examples. The first illumines many a marriage situation with compassion and tenderness. The second records

a moment of peace and beauty that will recur potentially
for ever.

The Way of It

With her fingers she turns paint
into flowers, with her body
flowers into a remembrance
of herself. She is at work
always, mending the garment
of our marriage, foraging
like a bird for something
for us to eat. If there are thorns
in my life, it is she who
will press her breast to them and sing.

Her words, when she would scold,
are too sharp. She is busy
after for hours rubbing smiles
into the wounds. I saw her,
when young, and spread the panoply
of my feathers instinctively
to engage her. She was not deceived,
but accepted me as a girl
will under a thin moon
in love's absence as someone
she could build a home with
for her imagined child.

R. S. Thomas

July Evening

A bird's voice chinks and tinkles
Alone in the gaunt reedbed –
  Tiny silversmith
Working late in the evening

I sit and listen. The rooftop
With a quill of smoke stuck in it
  Wavers against the sky
In the dreamy heat of summer.

Flowers' closing time: bee lurches
Across the hayfield, singing
   And feeling its drunken way
Round the air's invisible corners.

And grass is grace. And charlock
Is gold of its own bounty.
   The broken chair by the wall
Is all of immortal landscapes.

Something has been completed
That everything is part of.
   Something that will go on
Being completed forever.

Norman MacCaig

We take a further step when we realize that the poet has expressed things we were only vaguely aware of, attitudes perhaps that we might not have formed consciously had it not been for the poet's clearing up obscurities in ourselves. This poem, for instance, like Blake's, looks at babyhood, but this time from the point of view of mother and mother's mother, and with deceptive lightheartedness sharply focuses their rival responses, and their relationship with one another:

Infant Song

Don't you love my baby, mam,
Lying in his little pram,

Polished all with water clean,
The finest baby ever seen?

   Daughter, daughter, if I could
   I'd love your baby as I should,

   But why the suit of signal red,
   The horns that grow out of his head,

   Why does he burn with brimstone heat,
   Have cloven hooves instead of feet,

LANGUAGE

Fishing hooks upon each hand,
The keenest tail that's in the land,

Pointed ears and teeth so stark
And eyes that flicker in the dark?

Don't you love my baby, mam?

Dearest, I do not think I can,
I do not, do not think I can.

Charles Causley

Along with the pleasures of recognition goes that of contact, almost communion, with other human beings whom we feel we would like. They may be thousands of years away, like the author of this old Chinese poem on the common fate of man:

A Funeral Song

The dew on the shallot,
How quickly it dries!
The dew that's dried
Will fall again tomorrow.
The man that's died
Will never return again.

Chinese folk song of the Han dynasty

Or they may be thousands of miles away, like the singer of this 'Song while giving birth' from the pygmy people of Africa:

My heart is joyful,
My heart takes wing in singing,
Under the trees of the forest,
The forest our dwelling and our mother.
In my net I have taken
A little, a very little bird.
My heart is caught in the net,
In the net with the bird.

Though this is a translation from the language of a culture very different from ours, we feel in reading it that here is a human being experiencing the same joys and sorrows that complicate our own lives. We sense that the roots of our common human-ness go wide and deep; very much like Europeans, the pygmies turn to poetry in moments of crisis or when strongly moved. Literature, from popular songs to the Bible, provides the channels in which can flow the powerful feelings roused by the great events of life. At such times grief and suffering and elation are tempered by the knowledge that others too have experienced and overcome them. Thus poetry and drama help us to come to terms with living; they give us the material on which to decide that some experiences are more valuable than others.

Drama

While poetry, prose and drama have elements in common, dramatic writing cannot realise its full potential through reading alone. For a play to shed its full light and supply warmth and driving force, the power of the dramatist must be generated by actors, and the charge transmitted to an audience capable of receiving it. It is possible for a script to read well and yet not to act well; but a play which is successful on the stage will always prove of interest on the printed page, though not necessarily as 'literature' in the narrower sense.

George. Time for bed.
Martha. Yes.
George. Are you tired?
Martha. Yes.
George. I am.
Martha. Yes.
George. Sunday tomorrow – all day.
Martha. Yes. (A long silence between them) Did you . . . did you . . . have to?
George (pause). Yes.
Martha. It was . . ? You had to?

George (pause).   Yes.
Martha.   I don't know.
George.   It was . . . time.
Martha.   Was it?
George.   Yes.
Martha (pause).   I'm cold.
George.   It's late.

from *Who's Afraid of Virginia Woolf?* by Edward Albee

This extract has little in common with either prose or poetry and cannot be assessed as literature on the page. It depends for its validity entirely upon the timing and inflexions of the spoken word. It illustrates a comment of Peter Brook's:

A word is an end-product which begins as an impulse, stimulated by attitude and behaviour which dictates the need for expression. This process occurs inside the dramatist, and is repeated inside the actor; for both the word is a small visible portion of a gigantic unseen formation.   (*The Empty Space*)

The gaps between the fragments of dialogue have to be bridged by a concentration of understanding on the actor's part in order to convey meaning to the audience.

[Estragon has said 'Let us try and converse calmly, since we are incapable of keeping silent'.]
Vladimir.   You're right, we're inexhaustible.
Estragon.   It's so we won't think.
Vladimir.   We have that excuse.
Estragon.   It's so we won't hear.
Vladimir.   We have our reasons.
Estragon.   All the dead voices.
Vladimir.   They make a noise like wings.
Estragon.   Like leaves.
Vladimir.   Like sand.
Estragon.   Like leaves.
(Silence)
Vladimir.   They all speak together.

Estragon.	Each one to itself.
(Silence)	
Vladimir.	Rather, they whisper.
Estragon.	They rustle.
Vladimir.	They murmur.
Estragon.	They rustle.
(Silence)	

from *Waiting for Godot* by Samuel Beckett

Some of the poetry of this extract is accessible even to a reader by virtue of Beckett's use of imagery; and the rhythm inherent in the lines also makes its effect from the page. While in performance this piece will rely upon timing and inflexion, and concentration of understanding for its fullest effect, the writing is memorable for itself.

Dramatised fiction

The two extracts just quoted are examples of pure drama, conceived and written for performance in the same way that a novel is conceived and written for the private individual reader. Sometimes the two forms come together. The world's great novels have supplied marvellous material for TV and the cinema, and some extremely interesting and impressive interpretations have been made. But we do need to stress that the visual form, however faithfully the producers try to keep to the spirit of the original, is not and cannot be the same thing. The verbal and the visual are different in their operation and effects, and when they work together in the drama the results can be wonderful. A screen version lasting a couple of hours may be more gripping, get more dramatic and scenic results, be more realistic and (in the case of weak novels) actually be a more satisfying experience than the original prose story of 300 pages. But it will not be the same. A good novelist, like D. H. Lawrence, knows exactly what he is doing; he has chosen the medium because it is the best way of getting across his vision of life and its potentialities. Imaginative language does more than just state a plot and describe character. It does a great deal for the reader, but leaves a great deal to him too, for it sets his mind working so that he can play his part in the contract, the co-operation between reader and writer. TV, like the illustrations to a novel, does a lot for us over a limited area; it gives us one sharp clear aspect against the novel's dozens of facets. The visual version presents to us a particular set of actors, their dress, expression, movement, behaviour; we are often given a wonderfully vivid and complete living picture, but it is a picture which does everything for us; we are not given the stimulus that written words offer to the reader who co-operates fully and fills out the framework for himself. The film version leaves no room for doubt; it is clear and decisive; all the people who watch it are looking at the same thing, however much their responses may differ. And what they are seeing is the producer's picture, not the novelist's. Again, most watchers when comfortably settled for an evening's entertainment see the play right through. But with a novel in book form scores of responses are possible. It takes much longer, and therefore demands more effort, perseverance, stamina, even a trained habit of reading. The novel has plenty of room and a long time to set up its effects, skilfully devised to hold the reader's interest. For most novels require several sessions; the reader may not be in a position or in a mood to read a work steadily and may drop the whole thing till he feels like continuing. The reader sits in silence, alone with the author and his characters; he *must* use his imagination if he is to enjoy what the novelist's imagination has prepared for him.

Theatre or film?

The cinema and television are specialised forms of entertainment evolved by modern technology. They can present art forms as valid as the older art forms of the novel and the stage play. But a TV or film production, even when based on a novel or a play, has its own distinct aims, methods, even audiences sometimes – though it is significant that a successful film will always produce more readers for the book it is taken from. On the whole the more powerful a work of imagination the original novel or play is, the less successfully it can be adapted for TV or the cinema so as to convey anything of the author's vision. Shakespeare's tragedy *Macbeth* has been presented on film and on the television screen many times, each attempt capturing something of the play, but losing much as well. A primarily visual version can reduce one of the world's great plays to a run-of-the-mill magazine piece, exploiting sex and violence for commercial ends. Both elements are there in *Macbeth*, but in their place and seen in perspective; the audience or reader is left with the clear impression that violence breeds violence, and utterly destroys the character of the person who puts his trust in it as surely as it destroys the bodies of his victims. Like all great works of art *Macbeth* is a disturbing play. It confronts us with, and makes us re-think, a number of things, among them the fact that violence is infinitely corrupting, destroying the humanity of those who enjoy it; such people are literally sub-animal as well as sub-human. A film that exploits the violence in the play to provide a commercially successful spectacle is bound to distort and impoverish Shakespeare's vision, and to lose in the process the insights into our common humanity that he shares with us.

Commercial pressures

As we have shown, it is possible under the plea of bringing Shakespeare up-to-date or making him 'relevant to our times' to exploit certain aspects of his work and thereby seriously distort his artistic aims. It is not an accident that under Roman Polanski's direction *Macbeth* is made into yet another display of screened violence and eroticism rather than an artistic whole, a dramatic poem. What is noticeable here is that as visual spectacle is stressed – and the cinema and television have resources for this purpose undreamed of before this century – so language gets pushed into the background. The expressive and emotive resources of language are immense, almost inexhaustible; but they make considerable demands on the listener or reader who really wants to tap this potential. He or she becomes an active participant in the creative process initiated by the writer. Such strenuous involvement is alien to the world of popular – or 'pop' – entertainment; indeed, the commercial exploiters of the universal appetites for sex and violence rely on a passively receptive mass public, whose resistance or inertia must be overcome by increasing the dose – by ever more explicit sexual display or more crude and horrific acts of violence. This is why attempts to equate works of art like *Macbeth* with certain aspects of our culture are bound to fail; they pull in opposite directions, and in the process literature as we understand it disappears. Of course, the language is still used, but often in very limited or restricted modes, and generally subservient to the all-powerful visual images. This visual dominance, generated primarily by television, can be seen also in popular magazines and in newspapers, particularly the tabloids with their almost obligatory full-length or full frontal nudes, and their predigested gobbets of comment or chat couched in language that makes minimum demands on their readers. The borderline between such commercialised forms of literature and overtly commercial advertising is a shifting and tenuous one, and it is interesting to see with what technical sophistication the two are interwoven, both in television and in journalism. Many regular TV watchers will confess that the images and the doggerel jingle of the advertisements are more memorable than the programmes they interrupt; the American remedial education series *The Electric Company* frankly acknowledges it by incorporating many of the techniques of TV commercials in the programmes, and has been remarkably successful as a result. One has only to pick up any newspaper colour supplement to see the same process at work. A characteristic issue will contain two-fifths editorial material to three-fifths advertising, and it is often hard to distinguish the advertising from the rest, both drawing on similar techniques of presentation and persuasion.

The pop music phenomenon follows similar trends. However here – apart from popular television programmes like *Top of the Pops*, where spectacle becomes at least as important as sound – we are in an oral or aural environment. One might therefore expect language to play a more important part; all vital literature, after all, has its origins in the spoken or sung language and is continually revitalised by being heard as well as seen on the page. Pop music is an immense and varied field and it is difficult to generalise safely about it. There is no doubt that more people hear more music than ever before. Electronic techniques in recording, in the mass-production of records and cassettes, and in the manufacture of cheap and efficient reproducers, while they have made pop music instantly available, have also interposed barriers between performers and audience that make it difficult to see it as a genuinely popular art-form in the way that plays were in Shakespeare's day, or folk-songs in country districts up to a century ago. Pop songs, reflecting the isolation of much present-day life, tend to reiterate the obvious topics, ringing the changes on 'love', loneliness, nostalgia, with a drugging monotony. Many, perhaps most of the lyrics are simple and innocuous:

> You're my day, you're my night,
> When you're beside me it's all right;
> You're all the golden apples growing on my tree:
> I'm the island, you're the open sea.
>
> Do you remember the golden days
> When hand in hand we walked the same maze
> Of city streets . . .

LANGUAGE

> Day-time friends and night-time lovers,
> Hoping no-one else discovers;
> They don't want to hurt the others . . .

Sometimes a harsher note is struck:

> What do you do when you fall in love?
> You only get lies, and pain and sorrow.

Or even a wry realism:

> What do you get when you kiss a guy?
> You get a germ and catch pneumonia.

These are only random samples. The technological phenomenon of virtual saturation, twenty-four hours a day, by
pop music means that anyone who tunes in or visits a
record shop can find something to respond to at this level.
For much of it the words are unimportant and often inaud-
ible. The pop group or singer and the recording techni-
cians produce a processed package in which electronically
manipulated sounds, usually with a druggingly repetitive
beat, combine to provide an aural experience or background that is acceptable because it is familiar and easy on
the ear, to be talked through or enormously amplified in a
disco. The distance between the minimal demands made
by language as used in pop music and the more discrimin-
ating response demanded by literature in the forms that
we believe are significant is well demonstrated by the
following poems. Both set out to portray facets of our
commercial environment. Both, by their control of language, manage to present also an interpretation or a
comment on what they are describing:

Executive

I am a young executive. No cuffs than mine are cleaner;
I have a Slim-line brief-case and I use the firm's Cortina.
In every roadside hostelry from here to Burgess Hill
The maîtres d'hotel all know me well and let me sign the bill.

READING AND DISCRIMINATION

You ask me what it is I do. Well, actually, you know,
I'm partly a liaison man and partly P.R.O.
Essentially I integrate the current export drive,
And basically I'm viable from ten o'clock till five.

For vital off-the-record work – that's talking transport-wise –
I've a scarlet Aston-Martin – and does she go? She flies!
Pedestrians and dogs and cats – we mark them down for slaughter.
I also own a speed-boat which has never touched the water.

She's built of fibre-glass, of course, I call her 'Mandy-Jane'
After a bird I used to know – No soda, please, just plain –
And how did I acquire her? Well to tell you about that
And to put you in the picture I must wear my other hat.

I do some mild developing. The sort of place I need
Is a quiet country market town that's rather run to seed.
A luncheon and a drink or two, a little *savoir faire* –
I fix the Planning Officer, the Town Clerk and the Mayor.

And if some preservationist attempts to interfere
A 'dangerous structure' notice from the Borough Engineer
Will settle any buildings that are standing in our way –
The modern style, sir, with respect, has really come to stay.

John Betjeman

A Polished Performance

Citizens of the polished capital
    Sigh for the towns up country,
And their innocent simplicity.

People in the towns up country
    Applaud the unpolished innocence
Of the distant villages.

Dwellers in the distant villages
    Speak of a simple unspoilt girl,
Living alone, deep in the bush.

Deep in the bush we found her,
    Large and innocent of eye,
Among gentle gibbons and mountain ferns.

LANGUAGE

Perfect for the part, perfect,
　Except for the dropsy
Which comes from polished rice.

In the capital our film is much admired,
　Its gentle gibbons and mountain ferns,
Unspoilt, unpolished, large and innocent of eye.

D. J. Enright

These, like others in this book, are examples of language insisting on being taken seriously. For this to be possible the writers have to make their own position clear, have to come clean in a way that most lyrics of pop music don't or can't. This is not to deny that some pop singers succeed in resisting the commercial pressures and make music and sing their words from conviction, not merely for gain. The immense popularity of Bob Dylan, for instance, was first a genuine response to a genuine artist; and the relative cheapness of recording means that there are still opportunities for individuals to break into the pop scene with disturbing effect in spite of big business. Where this happens we can recognise language at work dynamically. The novelist Franz Kafka said when he was twenty: 'If the book we are reading does not wake us, as with a fist hammering on our skull, why then do we read it? . . . A book must be an ice-axe to break the sea frozen inside us.' The easy lyrics and stock responses of pop songs, and the impoverished language that accompanies most of the screened representations of violence, if accepted uncritically and not recognised for what they are, can make it more difficult to respond fully in the way Kafka describes.

Literature benefits the individual, but to society at large as well the ability to send clear messages is essential, both in the small change of daily living and in the larger dealings of nations. Medicine and science and engineering provide examples of successful communication, but elsewhere there is much wasted effort – in business, politics and the exchange of knowledge and beliefs. From the instructions on a fire-extinguisher upwards we need clarity – in directions, laws, and technical reports, for examples. Where the reader expects plain communication and gets it, there is no difficulty. But in fields such as politics, obscurity may be intentional; so that it is important not only to understand what the author says and the implications, but also to be aware of what he is leaving out, and of his intentions. He may be writing not just to give us balanced information but to slant our minds by providing a biased selection of facts; or he may be merely trying to set up a verbal smokescreen. If we are to blot out poverty and crime we need balanced facts, logical thought and cool discussion, as well as a passionate desire to lessen human suffering. Instead we find different methods at work: argument by misleading analogy: 'war is nature's pruning hook'; the use of abstractions to blunt the cutting edge of reality: 'dissident elements will be eliminated'; words like 'democracy' and 'freedom' with shifting meanings capable of supporting almost any argument; and finally slogans and emotionally charged expressions like 'red', 'blackleg' and 'fascist'.

The printed word is everywhere today, and in self-defence we tend to develop habits of reading without close attention. As a result, on the one hand we may find it difficult to understand and respond fully to Shakespeare, whose audience was accustomed to giving close aural attention and had powers of perception and retention that we have forgotten. At the other extreme we may become victims of various kinds of propaganda and advertising, which can only be seen for what it is when we learn to detect the writers' real aims, however cunningly concealed. At every level of written communication between these two extremes there are inadequacies, misunderstandings and obscurities to be faced. This is why we need not just the ability to read on the surface, but also some of the skill that the writers themselves employ. In the pages that follow we offer a technique of reading.

CHAPTER 2

A TECHNIQUE OF READING

In the pages that follow we offer a technique of reading that we believe will help anyone to understand to the full most types of the printed word. It is not the only method, but we know from experience that it has been useful to many readers. If everyone could read better, that is with a fuller understanding of the processes at work, millions might not be spent on advertising, the standard of political discourse and of committee work would be higher, journalism would be more responsible, and bad novels less lucrative. The quality of our living is affected by what we read; to read with discrimination and full understanding helps us to live more richly.

Our main concern in this book is with imaginative writing, and most of the examples we offer for assessment are from imaginative prose, poetry and drama. This is because in the best of such writing language is capable of realising its fullest potential. Moreover, the range of imaginative literature is as wide as life itself. Within it you will find all levels of response from the most flippant or casual expressions to the profoundest statements of man. Once you feel confident to assess such writing, to recognise when it is honest and effective, when and how it fails to achieve its aims, you are not likely to be hoodwinked by the tricks of advertising copy-writers or at the mercy of other unscrupulous practitioners with words.

Two uses of language: getting at meaning

1st speaker. There's a little dog in the garden.
2nd speaker. Oh, it's that flea-bitten cur from Number
  9. I wish she'd keep her rotten mongrel under control.

The word 'dog' in this dialogue has a plain straightforward meaning, to indicate a particular creature in a particular place; it is used almost scientifically. Because of this we accept the descriptive epithet 'little' as intended in the same way, to convey information. (It could be argued that the speaker might 'colour' the information a little by her tone of voice; we should need a sound recording to know this.) In the second speech 'cur' and 'mongrel' are used quite differently; the aim is to express the speaker's feelings about the event, and perhaps to involve the listener's sympathy. Speaker 1 gives us information; speaker 2 gives a twist to it. 'Cur' and 'mongrel' are emotionally toned; because of this we wouldn't bother to ascertain whether the dog really had fleas any more than we might speculate on its state of rotten-ness. The epithets merely reinforce the feeling.

A crowd threatens trouble, and a bystander says: 'Better call the police.' When they arrive one of the mob shouts: 'Here comes the fuzz!' 'Police' is used objectively or scientifically, 'fuzz' because of its associations carries an emotional charge. (If you have read the last few sentences with understanding you will recognise that we have shown our distaste for the emotive term 'fuzz' by changing a single word. What is it?)

Test this distinction for yourself. Some of the following expressions are relatively uncoloured by emotion, while others indicate strong feelings. For each provide two versions, one in the alternative form of the two we have distinguished, the other providing a second but different emotional colouring. Here is an example: (a) four or five adolescent boys (scientific); (b) a gang of teenage louts (emotional – anti); (c) a friendly-looking bunch of lads (emotional – pro).

1. A cool breeze fanned my cheek.
2. We were delayed for half an hour.
3. Why hang on to that heap of junk? (referring to a car)
4. I wouldn't be seen dead with that down-at-heel tramp.
5. My aunt is arriving tomorrow.

Everyone employs both kinds of language every day; there are times and occasions for both. A pair of lovers will not easily express their feelings in objective scientific language. On the other hand a chemist doing an experiment must use precise and unemotional language, otherwise he might blow the place up. Imaginative literature will naturally make use of emotionally charged language. Look again at the piece by Robert Burns quoted in Chapter One (p. 14). As a scientific statement the poem is worthless because from a scientific point of view no human being resembles a rose. Yet the images of the poem successfully convey the truth sensed by the lover that the girl has the freshness, delicacy and vigour of a rose, the joyful sweetness and absolute rightness of a well-played appealing tune.

Another appropriate place for emotive language is in public speaking. But for every good use of eloquence there are as many instances of the misuse of emotionally coloured language to obscure clear thinking, or to distort an audience's or a reader's view of the truth by stirring up feeling, especially in political matters and in advertising. Once one is aware of these two different kinds of language one soon learns to recognise where emotive words are justified and where they are misplaced.

Newspaper colour supplements are known to be a very effective advertising medium; consequently they include excellent specimens of emotive language. Consider the following advertisement (it may be best to read it aloud):

The month is June . . . The slopes of the Rhine and the Mosel are now pleasurably scented by the flowering vines. In all the vineyards sunburnt women, men and young people are intently busy tending their plants. Every hour's attention now will earn its reward in the October harvest. It is a time to spray the vines against pests and leaf diseases and to pray for sun, sun and more sun to nurture the flourishing shoots and to warm the very roots in the soil. In June, the wine is Oktober . . . Goldener Oktober . . . Cool, clear, light-hearted white wines from Germany.

Advertiser's copy usually has two aims, which may at times conflict. The first, of course, is to persuade people to buy the product; and the language of persuasion, as we have seen, is usually emotive. However, many – though not all – advertisements also aim to inform their readers about the product. Because their prime business is to sell, advertisers will usually be highly selective in the information they present, and not too particular about the scientific accuracy of the language it is couched in. An interesting way to prove this is to compare a manufacturer's description of his product, for example a washing-machine, or a hi-fi 'music centre', with a comparative report on it in the Consumers' Association magazine *Which?* In the advertisement quoted above both aims – informing and persuading are clearly seen. The manner in which the information is presented is a part of the persuasive technique. For instance, one *could* present one item of information thus: 'In June the vines are sprayed against pests and diseases.' Try setting out, in as few and as 'scientific' words as possible, the rest of the information in the passage. We know that if the advertisement did no more than state such information it would fail in its prime aim. So the factual element becomes merely a peg on which to hang the highly-coloured description leading up to the name of the product – itself chosen for its emotive charge. Notice in particular the effect of 'pleasurably scented', 'sunburnt women . . .', 'tending', 'earn its reward', 'to warm the very roots'. Read passively and uncritically, as most colour supplements *are* read, the advertisement will tend to induce a feeling of well-being and confidence, and that in turn makes it more likely that the name of the product will have pleasurable associations when next seen on the shelves of the off-licence. Such writing aims to engage the reader's feelings, not out of conviction, but to persuade him to buy one brand-name rather than another. You will find other examples of persuasive writing in Chapter Four (exx. 1C., 18).

At the other extreme comes true scientific writing. Here facts are presented without feeling, the aim being simply to convey information with clarity and precision:

A TECHNIQUE OF READING

Richard Boyle (1627–1691) discovered that in a given quantity of gas at a given temperature and pressure, pressure is inversely proportional to volume. Later Boyle's Law, $P^1V^1 = P^2V^2$, was combined with Charles' Law, making $PV = RT$. But Van der Waal showed that it was obtained only by neglecting inter-molecular attractions and the actual size of the molecules, and so corrected it to $(P + \frac{a}{V^2})(V-b) = RT$.

In a different context the word 'neglecting' could carry a considerable emotive charge. Here it is as cool and detached as the rest of the passage. However, writing that at first impression seems straight reporting may turn out to be warm with enthusiasm or coloured by other feeling. Where, for example, would you place this account of activities on the Stock Exchange on a scale between the extremes of scientific detachment and emotional involvement?

Most long-dated stocks recorded a rally of $\frac{1}{16}$, but movement in other British funds was erratic. Funding $8\frac{1}{2}$s regained $\frac{1}{8}$; Consols lost ground. Vigorous appreciation in certain South African mines was one of the cheerful features. A spurt of 7 hoisted Oldburgs to 84p, while the 10% prefs jumped 3 to 98 and B.A.N.S. moved briskly up to 220. South American stocks were generally reactionary, and there was some sagging on the rails. Most air lines were buoyant.

(Make up your mind about it before you read on.)
Although one might expect so mathematical a topic as the rises and falls in share values to be dealt with in fairly objective terms, the choice of words here tells us that the writer's feelings, and, he assumes, those of his readers, are in favour of plenty of activity with prices increasing. Hardly one of the changes is recorded in neutral terms.

In the wine advertisement the aim was to sell the product by expressing and stimulating feeling; in the scientific passage the intention was to record facts, to transmit information, to convey sense. We have here three useful terms to describe elements of meaning in language. Anything uttered or written has an INTENTION or aim; in most, though not in all, the speaker or writer presents items for consideration – the SENSE; and in many cases the FEELING of the speaker/writer about his subject is evident, whether genuine or simulated. A fourth aspect of total meaning is TONE. Although this term might seem to apply solely to the spoken language it usefully defines a fourth element in the total effect even of written English, i.e. the writer's attitude to his readers or audience. We need to be sure what a writer is getting at, what his intention is in writing at all. It may not be as obvious as one might think, particularly if it is in the writer's interest to conceal his real aim (e.g. of persuading you to spend money) by skilfully manipulating the other elements of meaning.

The writer's intention in the following passage (it is by the eighteenth-century historian Edward Gibbon) involves a subtle use of irony. Ostensibly he is defending the Christians, supporting the claim of the disciples to have performed miracles, and agreeing with St Mark that the Crucifixion was followed by three hours' darkness:

But how shall we excuse the supine inattention of the pagan and philosophic world to those evidences which were presented by the hand of Omnipotence, not to their reason, but to their senses? During the age of Christ, of his apostles, and of their first disciples, the doctrine which they preached was confirmed by innumerable prodigies. The lame walked, the blind saw, the sick were healed, the dead were raised, daemons were expelled, and the laws of Nature were frequently suspended for the benefit of the church. But the sages of Greece and Rome turned aside from the aweful spectacle, and, pursuing the ordinary occupations of life and study, appeared unconscious of any alterations in the moral or physical government of the world. Under the reign of Tiberius, the whole earth, or at least a celebrated province of the Roman Empire, was involved in a preternatural darkness of three hours. Even this miraculous event, which ought to have excited the wonder, the curiosity, and the devotion of mankind, passed without notice in an age of science and history.

(Decline and Fall of the Roman Empire, chapter XV)

Underlying the apparent concern at the indifference of the pagan world to the miraculous events recorded in the New Testament is a veiled but unmistakable scepticism, conveyed almost entirely by the ironic *tone*. Note the effect of such statements as '. . . the laws of Nature were frequently suspended for the benefit of the church', '. . . the whole earth, or at least a celebrated province of the Roman Empire . . .' After such clues a skilful reader can readily interpret the final sentence 'Even this miraculous event . . .' etc. in terms of the author's scepticism. Passages of this kind are often misunderstood because such clues are not taken up, and consequently the true intention is not appreciated. Further examples relating to this important link between the two aspects of meaning, tone and intention, are given Chapter Four (exx. 34, 35, 41B, 57).

We can see already that it is difficult to separate out the different aspects of meaning. The clue to Gibbon's true intention here lies in his tone. Nevertheless, because he is an historian, his wider aim will also be to convey *sense*, to chronicle the events as well as to comment on or interpret them. A short passage like the example given is not sufficient to illustrate this clearly. What we have to learn to recognise is which elements of meaning are dominant, and whether the circumstances justify that dominance which could lead to the suppression or distortion of other elements. Thus *feeling* may distort *sense* (as in the example on p. 37), or the *tone* may change the *intention*. In order to grasp clearly the distinction between these four elements, Sense, Intention, Feeling, Tone (use the word they make – SIFT – as a reminder that we are learning to 'sift' out the true meaning), it is worth looking for examples in our daily language experience. Voices will often reveal tone and feeling on television or radio – think of the disc-jockeys' characteristic modes of speech, or the TV compères'. Take even a simple greeting like 'Good morning'. The aim or intention is to maintain friendliness or promote goodwill, or just to keep in touch; *sense* hardly comes into it, a point made clear by pretending misunderstanding when we reply (as though to convey sense *were* the prime intention) 'What's good about it?' if it happens to be pouring with rain.

Rhythm

Our understanding of literature depends to a great extent on our response to it. As we have seen from our discussion of TONE this is a complex matter, involving both intellect and emotions. If we take a dislike to a writer we are not in a frame of mind to give him the attention he requires for a full appreciation of what he is saying. If we like and respect him, he is a good way towards achieving his aim. One of the most deep-seated elements of language is *rhythm*. An accomplished writer knows this, is himself responsive to it, and can control it in such a way as to give force, coherence and appeal to his poem or his prose.

What then is this powerful ally? Rhythm consists of sound patterns in time. At the very simplest level we tend to group successive sounds while hearing them, and to derive pleasure from doing so. A clock may tick at a uniform pace and loudness, but we hear it as *tick*-tock, with as it were a dominant and a subservient sound. A train's wheels may drum over the rails in repeated groups of four; we hear them as ˇ ˇ ˇ ′, with a stress on the final sound. Speech similarly falls into *stress patterns*; one only has to hear a foreigner – an Indian, for instance, whose language is relatively unaccented – speaking English to realise how much we depend on recognising them for our understanding of language. Moreover, variations in stress pattern can alter radically the meaning of what is being said. Consider the following syllables:

I aimed at the centre.

They form a simple unit of rhythm. Used as a flat state-ment it would contain two stresses — I aim′ed at the cen′tre. The next syllable in importance to these two is the first word 'I'. The two link words 'at the' and the unac-cented second syllable of 'centre' would not in normal usage be stressed. But even in such a simple group we find many possible variations. A heavy stress on 'aimed' would imply that I didn't achieve my aim. Transfer the heavy stress to 'I' and we recognise that the speaker is contrast-ing his behaviour with someone else's. Try it for yourself. How many different meanings can rhythmic changes give to this expression:

Are you coming on this bus?

The placing of stresses, and their relative weights, determine rhythm patterns. In language these patterns tend to form short rhythmic units separated by *pauses*. Sometimes — more frequently in prose than in poetry — the pauses are diminished or even over-ridden in the interest of a continuous rhythmic flow; but they are always felt by speaker or reader, and contribute import-antly to the meaning. As in music, sound is defined by silence. The length, frequency and position of pauses form the other important element in rhythm. In writing we sometimes need punctuation to ensure that our readers place the pauses correctly: I have just used it thus after the word 'music'. In poetry line-endings can — though they do not invariably do so — serve the same purpose. Let us consider a little more closely how such an organically oral and aural element in language as rhythm can be conveyed through the written word. When we read we 'hear' the words. Less practised readers can often be seen mouthing the words silently as they read. So we meet the writer half-way over rhythm. Nevertheless, there is often a large area of choice, as in the two examples we've just given you. In ordinary discourse, and in unengaged or merely utilitarian prose, this doesn't matter, so long as the rhythm is not left so uncertain as to distort or conceal the sense. The context of each rhythmic unit within the passage provides guidance enough. In more urgent or more imaginative writing rhythm becomes increasingly important, and our awareness of and response to it can affect our total understanding as well as our enjoyment to a considerable degree.

T. S. Eliot, in his poetry, shows himself particularly sensitive to rhythmic effects, whether in regular or free verse. D. W. Harding (*Words Into Rhythm*, 1976) gives a good example of his skill at the end of *The Hollow Men*. The poem concerns disillusionment, relating to the predicament of the Christian in the twentieth century.

Where, in a continuously flowing passage, there are alternative ways of handling the sub-units of rhythm, optional points of pause, the choice has to be made in accordance with the sense and feeling of that passage in relation to its context. We could – but most readers would not – take the last line of Eliot's 'The Hollow Men' as a sort of dactylic gallop[1] –

> Not with a   bang but a   whimper.

That might just be defended as emphasising the bitter nursery-rhyme quality of the line. But to bring out the contrast between 'bang' and 'whimper', and because of the stress pattern of 'This is the way the world ends', used three times over in the immediately preceding lines, we are virtually bound to phrase it

> Not with a bang   but a whimper.

Verse frequently makes use of regular repeated rhythmic patterns, called *metres*. Traditionally these have been classified according to stress pattern and numbers of syllables, the most common in English verse being:

iambus (adj. iambic) ˘ ′	anapaest (–ic) ˘ ˘ ′
trochee (trochaic) ′ ˘	dactyl (–ic) ′ ˘ ˘
spondee (spondaic) ′ ′	

---

[1] dactyl = a stressed syllable followed by two unstressed.

A TECHNIQUE OF READING

Much of Shakespeare's dramatic poetry uses a metre of

five iambic 'feet' as its basis; in fact this ten-syllabled (or decasyllabic) line, sometimes called an iambic pentameter [penta = five], constitutes the commonest of all English metres. Nevertheless, even in metred verse the rhythms of speech remain basic and inviolable. If a poet uses metre so insensitively as to obscure or distort speech rhythms we soon tire of the repetition; our ear becomes dulled and the effect is monotonous. What an established metre can do is to determine the choice between two or more available speech rhythms. This is because the pattern established by metrical repetition directs, almost without our being aware of it, the way we rhythmise the words. Another of D. W. Harding's examples will make this clear.

The statement 'She sat here in her chair' could be spoken quite naturally with two stresses – on 'sat' and 'chair', or perhaps on 'here' and 'chair'. But as a line in Hardy's poem it takes yet another stress pattern because of the metre established in the previous stanza:

> Here is the ancient floor,
> Footworn and hollowed and thin . . .
>
> She' sat here' in her chair' . . .

where the emphasis given to 'She' prepares for the antithesis with 'He' two lines later[2] . . . Metre chooses from the rhythmical alternatives the one that creates the metre.

However dominant or regular the metrical pattern it can never, in good poetry, work against natural speech rhythms. On the other hand, a poet fully alert to the rhythmic resources of language can employ metre subtly to enhance his effects. Let us look at a famous speech of Macbeth's, his response to the news that his wife is dead:

---

[2] See Chapter Four, ex. 9B for this poem in full.

> She should have died hereafter.
> There would have been a time for such a word –
> Tomorrow, and tomorrow, and tomorrow,
> Creeps in this petty pace from day to day
> To the last syllable of recorded time;
> And all our yesterdays have lighted fools
> The way to dusty death. Out, out, brief candle!
> Life's but a walking shadow, a poor player
> That struts and frets his hour upon the stage
> And then is heard no more. It is a tale
> Told by an idiot, full of sound and fury,
> Signifying nothing.

Apart from the short lines at the beginning and the end – both gaining something of their effect from their departure from the pentameter – the lines are recognisably iambic pentameters. Yet only four (lines 2, 6, 9 and 10) come anywhere near being 'regular', with alternating stresses. Of the remaining six five have an extra syllable, and all depart sharply from the iambic 'set'. What Shakespeare can do is to use our aroused expectation for the repeated pattern to direct our understanding of the emotions Macbeth is experiencing. Line 2 with its drugging regularity emphasised by the monosyllables conveys vividly his sense of hopelessness and despair, and leads into the thrice muttered 'Tomorr'ow' – three heavy stresses instead of the expected five. But here, because of the metre so drummed into us in the previous line, our ear tends to put stresses also on the link words 'and', which we would not do if it were prose. The effect is startling, weighing the line down almost physically with Macbeth's feeling that life is now merely a meaningless succession of days, and illustrating graphically the following line 'Creeps in *this* petty pace . . . .'. Shakespeare uses the iambic pattern again for a particular effect in line 9. 'Life' is seen as 'a poor player' – an actor like Macbeth himself (a characteristically Shakespearian piece of double-take) – but because he is unskilled all he can do is to 'strut and fret'[3], and the dull rhythm demonstrates his ineptitude. There is much more to discover in the subtle rhythmic effects of a passage like this, and the way they both direct and enhance our understanding. See if you can decide what rhythmic effects are achieved in lines 6 and 7, or 10 to 12.

Because rhythm depends on the shapes and patterns we are aware of when we speak, it is an equally powerful ally to poets writing unmetrical verse, and to novelists and other prose writers. There are always the elements of stress and pause, and of repetition. Here is one of Geoffrey Hill's *Mercian Hymns*, a series of thirty prose-poems in which he explores the sharply original idea of King Offa as 'the presiding genius of the West Midlands, his dominion enduring from the middle of the eighth century until the middle of the twentieth'. In this poem Offa becomes the twentieth-century business executive, but with curious lapses into childish memories and long-ings.

He adored the desk, its brown-oak inlaid with ebony,
 assorted prize pens, the seals of gold and base metal into which
 he had sunk his name.

It was there that he drew upon grievances from the people; attended
 to signatures and retributions; forgave the death-howls of his
 rival. And there he exchanged gifts with the Muse of History.

What should a man make of remorse, that it might profit his soul?
 Tell me. Tell everything to Mother, darling, and God bless.

He swayed in sunlight, in mild dreams. He tested the little pears.
 He smeared catmint on his palm for his cat Smut to lick. He wept,
 attempting to master *ancilla* and *servus*.

If we set out the second section as a more conventional stanza the increased rhythmic regularity becomes evident:

---

[3] The same term 'strut' is used by Hamlet to describe a poor actor.

47

It was there' that he drew' upon griev'ances from the peop'le;
Attend'ed to sig'natures and ret'ribut'ions;
Forgave' the death'-howls(') of his rival.
And there' he exchang'ed gifts' with the Muse' of His'tory.

The steadier beat helps to convey the picture of Offa
carrying out his habitual official functions. But the underlying irony evident from the beginning – 'He *adored* the
desk' – and informing the indifferent brutality of 'forgave
the death-howls' (a significant ripple marring the rhythmic
regularity at this point), is made clear in the overtly
Biblical rhythm employed at the opening of section three,
which gives way abruptly to the cosy 'Tell everything to
Mother, darling'. Geoffrey Hill chooses in this book to
dispense with both metre and verse-lines, yet his handling
of rhythm is as important as ever. We can no longer argue
either that rhythm in poetry depends on metre or variants
from it, or that free verse, being merely 'prose chopped
up', is in some way inferior. As D. W. Harding points
out: 'To complain that free verse is just prose chopped up
into lines ignores the fact that all the prose we ever read
is chopped up into lines; we rightly pay no attention to
them. But the line of free verse demands attention, not
as a typographical whim but as the outline of a rhythmical unit which interacts with other language patterns'
(p. 71).

We have discussed rhythm as a separate phenomenon
of language. Yet we need to remember that it can no
more be isolated in its effect than, say, colour can in a
picture. Take out the separate blobs of colour from a
picture and they become meaningless; see them as part of
the totality and they enhance our enjoyment. In prose, as
in verse, 'rhythms accord with, and enhance, expressions
of emotion and mood, the mournful, the gay, the fierce,
for instance. But the sense of the language is needed too:
if there is a language of rhythm alone it has a small
vocabulary; each pattern of rhythm can be appropriate to
a range of purposes one of which will be more narrowly

defined by the sense of the words and the context'
(D. W. Harding, p. 150).

To sum up: all rhythm in written English derives from speech. Our everyday speech is often hesitant, disjointed, repetitive, pieced out by gesture, facial expressions, intonation and volume. Because writing has none of these aids, rhythm has a larger part to play and needs to be controlled with greater sensitivity. Our dissatisfaction with some poetry and prose may stem from our subconsciously recognising rhythmic inadequacies – insensitive repetition, inappropriate sound-patterns (jaunty and quick where they should be sombre and slow-moving, or ponderous where they need to convey rapidity or lightness), or patterns set up by metre or less formal means then stumbled over so that one's legitimate expectations are disappointed. Conversely, our pleasure in fine poetry or felicitous prose will certainly owe something to our response to the appropriateness and variety of the rhythm. It is an important part of reading technique to learn to distinguish such qualities.

Imagery

We have now established a way of approaching the full meaning of any piece of writing, of learning how to SIFT out the meaning. We have also examined, and suggested ways of recognising, the effects of *rhythm*, one of the basic features of language. Another feature integral to language is *imagery*. We have seen that a writer's control of rhythm can influence our response to what he writes. Imagery, growing in a similar way from the very roots of language, can also play a large part in determining how writing affects us. For it starts where language itself starts: with our instinctive search for affinities or likenesses in trying to make sense of ourselves in our surroundings. Think how often when we are seeking information or enlightenment we ask 'What is X like?' We are asking for an image so that the new experience or the unfamiliar phenomenon can be grasped and assimilated, made our own, and thereby brought under control. (In his *Just So Story* 'How the first letter was written' Rudyard Kipling makes a provocative and entertaining guess at the metaphorical origins of the written language; the children's author Clive King takes the matter further in *The 22 Letters*.)

Let us consider two statements, the first by a poet, the second by a critic:

Every poetic image . . . is to some degree metaphorical. It looks out from a mirror in which life perceives not so much its face as some truth about its face.

(C. Day Lewis *The Poetic Image*)

A metaphor is the result of the search for a precise epithet. . . . Try to be precise, and you are bound to be metaphorical; you simply cannot help establishing affinities between all the provinces of the animate and the inanimate world.

(J. Middleton Murry *The Problem of Style*)

Before going further it will be as well to sort out a little the terms we shall be using here. The term *image* together with its abstract collective form *imagery* is the inclusive one, comprising all the examples and kinds of comparison we shall be discussing. Thus it embraces both *simile* and *metaphor*, and will include some kinds of *personification* as well as more specialised terms like paradox, metonymy, synecdoche, and Ruskin's useful coinage *pathetic fallacy*. An image need not, however, be contained in any one of these categories. Sometimes it may include several of them; sometimes it cannot be satisfactorily described by any of them. An image may be established through a single word (e.g. the word 'syllable' in the passage from *Macbeth* on page 46); alternatively it may consist of a full-length story like E. M. Forster's *The Machine Stops*, or George Eliot's *The Lifted Veil*; or a long poem like *The Waste Land*, by T. S. Eliot. It may even form the central shaping force of a non-fictional work: Geoffrey Moorhouse's travel book *The Fearful Void* is a good example, in which he describes his attempt to cross the Sahara desert. Because the words *image* and *imagery* do not have a suitable cognate epithet – the word 'imaginary' having quite a different connotation – we tend to use instead, when we need an epithet, the term *metaphorical*, so that it takes on rather wider significance than its noun *metaphor*. We see this in the two quotations just given. Later we shall be looking briefly at the way imagery relates to the more far-reaching concepts *symbol, allegory* and *myth*.

For the poet C. Day Lewis an image is a way of apprehending truth. Let us see how he puts this into practice:

> Lark, skylark, spilling your rubbed and round
> Pebbles of sound in air's still lake
>
> (from *The Ecstatic*)

The comparison is appreciated immediately, with a shock of realisation – 'Of course! A lark's song *is* like pebbles falling into water'. We recognise the truth of the analogy, and our newly awakened awareness gives us a pleasurable excitement. As we look closer we notice other things: the 'air', the blue arch of sky (we have to employ another image), *is* like a 'still lake'; the individual yet linked sounds of the lark's song *are* like a succession of pebbles 'spilled' into water. And the very sound of the words – lark/lake; *rubbed* an*d* roun*d*; pebble*s* of *s*ound in air'*s s*till – helps us to respond to this visual image describing an aural experience.

We see from this one example three essentials of imagery. It will always be *sensuous*, i.e. work through our physical senses; most frequently the sense of sight, but images can appeal to any or all the senses. 'The discrimination of sense-perception is the most active principle at work in refining language' (J. M. Murry). Secondly, it will aim at *precision*, exactness of description. Thirdly, there will often be an element of *shock* or surprise, that awakens us into a new alertness of response. This image, by the American poet Richard Eberhart, forms the opening of a poem called *The Return of Odysseus*:

> My disappointments, huge as capsized tugs,
> Pull no more the big ship of love.

Here the abstract 'disappointments' is made real by the surprising (and one might think 'unpoetical') 'capsized tugs'. As we assimilate the idea we respond to its appropriateness, its exact defining of what it seeks to convey with relation to the sea-bound Homeric myth of Odysseus' return.

A fourth ingredient in imagery takes us back to our four-fold definition of meaning, for it is *feeling*. Coleridge says:

Images, however beautiful . . . do not of themselves characterize the poet. They become proofs of original genius only as far as they are modified by a predominant passion; or by associated thoughts or images awakened by that passion.

C. Day Lewis, who quotes this, goes on to show that although imagery must be passionately felt by the poet it need not convey the feeling it embodies direct to the reader. Hence we may read or witness in the theatre an appalling tragedy like the disintegration of King Lear's personality, yet derive a deep pleasure from it.

Let us take our next example from this greatest play of Shakespeare's. Inevitably, it is a much more complex image or intertwined set of images. Lear, like other Shakespearian tragic heroes, finds a lucidity and perceptiveness in his madness that was denied him when he was 'sane'. In this scene he is talking with poor blinded Gloster, with Gloster's true son Edgar as a sensitive witness who recognises the king's 'reason in madness':

> Through tatter'd clothes small vices do appear;
> Robes and furr'd gowns hide all. Plate sin with gold
> And the strong lance of justice hurtless breaks;
> Arm it in rags, a pigmy's straw does pierce it.

Through the disillusioned and rejected father and monarch Shakespeare is expressing here vital truths, coloured with a tragic cynicism both by the speaker and by the dramatic circumstances. It is worth noting the economy of language. Try to capture the full meaning of Lear's observations in a paraphrase; you might start something like this:

In poor people, whose clothes may be torn and inadequate, we find it easier to detect sins which in the rich would be overlooked . . .

As soon as one attempts such botchery one realises the force and vision behind Shakespeare's image-cluster. Note the pathos inherent in the idea of 'vices' like bits of naked flesh appearing through holes in the tattered garments of paupers – an image that has gained impetus and significance throughout the play and was emblematically portrayed by the Fool in earlier scenes with Lear. Notice also the vivid immediacy of 'plate sin with gold', which conveys two sharply different ideas at the same time, fusing them together with shocking intensity. First there is the image of plates of steel armour tough enough to resist a lance thrust. But we also recognise the sham of gold plating a baser metal, which gives a new concreteness to the abstract 'sin'. This is followed by the paradox 'arm it in rags', which consequently carries greater force of meaning and gives a poignancy to the concluding image of the 'pigmy's straw' piercing the beggar's puny defences. You will find a similar richness of meaning in passages for closer study and analysis in Chapter Four (e.g. exx. 10, 13, 17B, 32B, 42, 47, 48A).

We need to distinguish clearly between imagery such as this and language used symbolically. A *symbol* is an actual concrete thing that is accepted as representing something of wider significance. The important word here is 'accepted'. An image cannot acquire symbolic potency until it is recognised to represent a collective response. Thus bread and wine can be accepted as symbols of body and blood only because, and only to the extent that, they coincide with the beliefs and practice of Christians. For non-Christians they remain images or metaphors, representing rather than symbolising Christ's body and blood.

READING AND DISCRIMINATION

Where a society is fragmented as ours is in the Western world symbolism tends not to be a very significant element in our language. Primitive or tribal societies find symbols for the forces of nature, for the seasons, for all manifestations of power that seem to be outside their control. It may be that we are learning to treat the discoveries of science and the products of technology symbolically. One thinks of many lines in the poetry of R. S. Thomas:

> . . . What word so explosive
> as that one Palestinian
> word with the endlessness of its fall-out?
>
> (from *Nuclear*)

> . . . You speak
> all languages and none,
> answering our most complex
> prayers with the simplicity
> of a flower, confronting
> us, when we would domesticate you
> to our uses, with the rioting
> viruses under our lens.
>
> (from *Praise*)

Here the images of the 'rioting viruses' and of nuclear fall-out – especially the latter which has been widely used metaphorically – acquire almost the validity of symbols for the 1970s. Perhaps it is no coincidence that R. S. Thomas is a priest and a deeply religious man (see ch. 4, ex. 42).

We have ranged briefly over the whole field of this very complex aspect of language. In our examples we have concentrated on poetry because it is in this form of literature that imagery is exploited to the full. Nevertheless it informs language in all its modes, even when used scientifically. One has only to think of Kekulé's day-dream referred to on p. 17.

A TECHNIQUE OF READING

The Resources of English

English has greater expressive resources than those of any other language; the main reason is the huge vocabulary acquired from other countries, often through war or invasion, during the fifteen centuries or so that it has been growing.

Anglo-Saxon, sometimes called Old English, has provided the core of our language – words dealing with the body, the seasons and the weather, the sea, the land, farming and vigorous action. Anglo-Saxon poetry, by using this 'word-hoard' (an Anglo-Saxon term) and by pointing the rhythm with alliteration rather than rhyme and metre, keeps close to the suppleness of speech. In fact all Anglo-Saxon poetry, like most poetry up to and including Shakespeare and much of it after that, was written primarily to be heard, and needed oral qualities even to survive. At first sight it looks on the page like a foreign language, but closer study reveals its kinship with today's English. Here is the opening of a fine anonymous poem called *The Seafarer*, together with Ezra Pound's translation. Pound catches the spirit of the poem by keeping close to the actual words, and because so many of these are still a part of our language he is able to make a fluent and convincing new poem. This is not so surprising when we note that in the first line, for instance, only one half-word, '–giedd', is totally unfamiliar.

> Mæg ic be mē *s*ylfum *s*ōðgied*d* wrecan,
> *s*īþas *s*ecgan,   hū ic ge*s*wincdagum
> *ea*rfoðhwīle   *o*ft þrōwade,
> *b*itre *b*rēostceare   ge*b*iden hæbbe,
> gecunnad in *c*ēole   *c*earselda fela,
> *a*tol ȳþa gewealc.   Þær mec *o*ft bigeat
> *nea*ro *n*ihtwaco   æt *n*acan stefnan,
> þonne hē be *c*lifum *c*nossað.   *C*alde geþrungen
> wæron *f*ēt mine   *f*orste gebunden,
> *c*aldum *c*lommum;   þær þā *c*eare seofedun
> *h*āt[e] ymb heortan;   *h*ungor innan slāt
> *m*erwērges *m*ōd.

55

> May I for my own self song's truth reckon,
> Journey's jargon, how I in harsh days
> Hardship endured oft.
> Bitter breast-cares have I abided,
> Known on my keel many a care's hold,
> And dire sea-surge, and there I oft spent
> Narrow nightwatch nigh the ship's head
> While she tossed close to cliffs. Coldly afflicted,
> My feet were by frost benumbed.
> Chill its chains are; chafing sighs
> Hew my heart round and hunger begot
> Mere-weary mood.

The Seafarer was written some time in the eighth century A.D. Some six centuries later the language – usually called Middle English to distinguish it from the earlier stage we have just been examining – had moved much closer to our English of today. The strength of the Anglo-Saxon heritage was still evident, particularly in the writing of William Langland, author of *Piers Plowman*, and in that remarkable anonymous romance *Sir Gawayn and the Green Knight*. Listen to this complaint of about 1450 against the noise of a local industry; the whole poem (about 20 lines) is near to the experience it conveys and brings the scene vividly to our ears and eyes:

> Swarte-smoked smethes, so smattered with smoke,
> Drive me to deth with den of there dintes:
> Swich noise on nightes ne herd men never,
> What knavene cry and clattering of knockes!

> (swarte – black; den – din; knavene – workmen's)

The fact that poetry can speak so directly to us across the centuries is one of the best indications of the rich resources now stored up in the language. The central 'maker' or poet in Middle English literature, Geoffrey Chaucer, demonstrates in his writings both his indebtedness to continuing English traditions and the greatly increased richness and variety brought to it by French, Italian, Latin and other foreign influences during his life-time. English has always had this sponge-like capacity to absorb and make its own the linguistic products of other cultures. It is particularly evident today, as we shall see later in this chapter in talking of it as the most influential world-language. Consequently English writers have had, and still have, the advantage of being able to use words carrying a powerful charge of associations, a resonance of unique power.

Here is just one example from thousands of the way novelists in this century make use of the 'memory-bank' they are working with. Virginia Woolf is describing a moment of almost elegiac calm, reflected in Mrs Dalloway's placid occupation:

Quiet descended on her, calm, content, as her needle, drawing the silk smoothly to its gentle pause, collected the green folds together and attached them, very lightly, to the belt. So on a summer's day waves collect, overbalance and fall; collect and fall; and the whole world seems to be saying 'that is all' more and more ponderously, until even the heart in the body which lies in the sun on the beach says too, that is all. Fear no more, says the heart. Fear no more, says the heart, committing its burden to some sea, which sighs collectively for all sorrows, and renews, begins, collects, lets fall. And the body alone listens to the passing bee; the wave breaking; the dog barking, far away barking and barking.

The mood is beautifully evoked and sustained, in the rhythm, in the sleepy repetitions, echoing the whole context of quiet familiar sounds. But Virginia Woolf also draws on a particular song of Shakespeare's that appropriately reinforces the mood: the dirge over the (believed) dead body of Imogen in Act IV of *Cymbeline*:

> Fear no more the heat o' th' sun,
>   Nor the furious winter's rages...

(See ch. 4, ex. 22)

Does it matter that we may not recognise the allusion when we read the novel? Probably not; a sensitive reader would respond to the tone as of a half-remembered tune. But it is interesting to see how for Virginia Woolf the resource is there to be drawn on. Shakespeare in his turn had done the same with the language as he found it, drawing on the Bible and the lively oral traditions connected with it, mystery and morality plays in particular, on folksong and the hidden wealth of proverbial wisdom, as well as more conventional literary sources. Here is another twentieth-century example, from an episode in T. S. Eliot's *Waste Land*. The 'young man carbuncular' has just left his woman; the poet comments:

> When lovely woman stoops to folly and
> Paces about her room again, alone,
> She smoothes her hair with automatic hand,
> And puts a record on the gramophone.
> 'This music crept by me upon the waters'

In the famous 'Notes on the Waste Land' Eliot gives us the sources of his two allusions here. In the first he refers back ironically to a song in Goldsmith's novel *The Vicar of Wakefield* (1766):

> When lovely woman stoops to folly,
>   And finds too late that men betray,
> What charm can soothe her melancholy,
>   What art can wash her guilt away?

implying a comparison between eighteenth- and twentieth-century attitudes to sexual behaviour. It may appear that the comparison is presented dispassionately, leaving the reader to make up his mind; but Eliot's cunning shift of metre from four- to five-foot iambs gives the rather superficial jingle of the novel an oddly disconcerting quality that is reinforced by the over-regular line 'And puts . . .' etc. The irony is compounded by the other allusion, which links the tinny sound of a gramophone in the girl's bed-sitter with Ariel's magical music on Prospero's island in Shakespeare's last play *The Tempest*.

Look again at Geoffrey Hill's prose-poem (p. 47). The

Anglo-Saxon simplicity of the language in the first part gives way in the second to a more latinate diction – 'signatures', 'retribution' – the words lending a sonority to the executive attitudes described, which is harshly interrupted by the Anglo-Saxon 'death-howls'. We noted the rhythmic effect of this, and of the biblical echo 'What should a man make of remorse . . .' tailing off into the formal emptiness of the parental 'God bless'. The conclusion of this poem comes as an apt reminder that the intensive study of Latin was until recently – and in many schools still is – regarded as a necessary part of education.

The 'English language' we have been discussing was the language that developed and formed the vernacular in the United Kingdom up to the 1930s. For a hundred years or so before that it had also been one of our more valuable exports – to the British colonies and dominions, and thus to North America in particular. During the last forty or fifty years the picture has become more confused. We can no longer talk in terms of exporting *our* language as though by the accident of living where it originated we had some kind of vested interest. Numerically far more non-British than British now speak English as their mother-tongue; it is the official medium for more than 500 million people all over the world. The cultural implications of this phenomenon are profound, and lie outside the scope of our theme, but any serious reader of English nowadays has to accept – and should accept with gratitude – that the next major English novelist, poet or playwright is as likely to live in America or Australia or Africa as in the United Kingdom. When in our twentieth century we read poetry by T. S. Eliot (American) or W. B. Yeats (Irish), drama by Bernard Shaw (Irish) or Athol Fugard (South African), novels by Patrick White (Australian) or Saul Bellow (American), we are as involved in English literature as with the work of John Donne or William Congreve or Jane Austen. Undoubtedly the language will continue to change, will continue to absorb new ideas and to generate new ways of expressing them. The speed and variety of the changes make it all the more necessary to learn to read with discrimination. Some of the passages chosen for closer study will reflect this important change by being drawn from the work of overseas writers. (See ch. 4, exx. 16, 23B, 27, 38, 41A, 46, 49B.)

A note on prose fiction

Much of what we have been saying so far has related particularly to poetry. People are less used to reading or hearing poetry today than they were in the past; no more than a century ago a long poem could become a best-seller, a state of affairs almost inconceivable today. So it is helpful to have guidance in approaching the reading of poetry. However, the same language processes are at work in all literary forms. A good novelist has to be as alert to the potentialities of imagery and rhythm as a poet, even though his or her mode of writing may permit a more leisurely and detailed treatment of the chosen theme.

Our main problem in a book of this kind when we discuss prose fiction is that its most important effects are cumulative, derived not from short and readily quotable passages but from the establishing and developing of ideas, characters and settings – all of them inter-related – over successive chapters or even books. Indeed, to quote and analyse short passages can be positively misleading. Passages full of detectable examples of imagery, rhythm, tone and so on may not convey a true impression of the work as a whole; and novels full of such passages may even be bad novels, however suitable for the dissecting table. A novel is the most private of literary forms. There have been attempts to break down this privacy, this one-to-one contact between writer and reader. One thinks of Charles Dickens's famous public readings from his own books, and of course in our own day there is the popularising of books by means of television, radio or film dramatisations. We have seen already in Chapter One how the latter may falsify or cheapen the novels they derive from.

When we settle down to read a novel we are entering into a relationship with the novelist. For hours, spread over days or even weeks, we are going to be in his or her company, subject to his or her view of life. If the novelist succeeds in convincing us of the reality of his created characters in their fictional surroundings, and in holding our interest in what happens to them, we voluntarily submit to his attitudes and accept his values, at least while we are reading the novel. It is an important part of the technique of reading to become aware of this; not to be a passive 'consumer' of novels – paperback publishers' lists and public libraries are full of commercial fiction churned out to cater for such uncritical customers – but to recognise what we are being asked to accept, to decide whether it accords with our sense of values or perhaps opens our mind to new possibilities, or whether the novel embodies a distorted, or partial, or morally unacceptable view of life.

This most central of critical concerns cannot be dealt with through excerpts short enough to be included in a book of this kind, and it would be misleading to pretend that it can. A negative example, so to speak, will illustrate the point. Thomas Hardy's novel *Jude the Obscure* concerns the intense, tempestuous and finally tragic love affair of Jude and his cousin Sue Bridehead. As the story unfolds we see how their backgrounds and social circumstances have so shaped their personalities that their relationship, based though it is on kinship and deep mutual affection, is doomed. This passage comes when Sue, unjustly punished in her teacher training college for having been out with Jude, has run away and come to Jude's lodgings for shelter. He has lent her some clothes to allow her soaked ones to dry, and they are engaged in conversation:

'Jude,' she said brightly . . . , 'will you let me make you a *new* New Testament, like the one I made for myself at Christminster?'
'O yes. How was that made?'
'I altered my old one by cutting up all the Epistles and Gospels into separate brochures, and re-arranging them in chronological

order as written, . . . Then I had the volume re-bound . . . Reading it afterwards made it twice as interesting as before, and twice as understandable.'

'H'm!' said Jude, with a sense of sacrilege.

'And what a literary enormity this is,' she said, as she glanced into the pages of Solomon's Song. 'I mean the synopsis at the head of each chapter, explaining away the real nature of that rhapsody. You needn't be alarmed: nobody claims inspiration for the chapter headings. Indeed, many divines treat them with contempt. It seems the drollest thing to think of the four-and-twenty elders, or bishops, or whatever number they were, sitting with long faces and writing down such stuff.'

Jude looked pained. 'You are quite Voltairean!' he murmured.

'Indeed? Then I won't say any more, except that people have no right to falsify the Bible! I *hate* such humbug as could attempt to plaster over with ecclesiastical abstractions such ecstatic, natural, human love as lies in that great and passionate song!' Her speech had grown spirited, and almost petulant at his rebuke, and her eyes moist. 'I *wish* I had a friend here to support me; but nobody is ever on my side!'

'But my dear Sue, my very dear Sue, I am not against you!' he said, taking her hand, and surprised at her introducing personal feeling into mere argument.

'Yes you are, yes you are!' she cried, turning away her face that he might not see her brimming eyes. 'You are on the side of the people in the Training School – at least you seem almost to be! What I insist on is, that to explain such verses as this: "Whither is thy beloved gone, O thou fairest among women?" by the note: *The Church professeth her faith* is supremely ridiculous!'

'Well then, let it be! You make such a personal matter of everything! I am – only too inclined just now to apply the words profanely. You know *you* are the fairest among women to me, come to that!'

'But you are not to say it now!' Sue replied, her voice changing to its softest tone of severity. Then their eyes met, and they shook hands like cronies in a tavern, and Jude saw the absurdity of quarrelling on such a hypothetical subject, and she the silliness of crying about what was written in an old book like the Bible.

[Chap. 4]

The topic here is straightforward, and we can get some idea of the nature of the relationship, with Sue in the lead, and her unselfconscious feminine charm beguiling Jude into condoning what he, as a future clergyman, secretly disapproves of in her approach to the Bible. Hardy is faithful to the emotional tempo of the scene: the way Sue, by getting worked up ('her speech had grown spirited, and almost petulant at his rebuke'), quite unconsciously becomes more attractive to Jude, so that their reconciliation, with its ironic 'like cronies in a tavern', has a piquant blend of companionship and love. Perhaps the most skilful touch is the reason given after this handshake for their respective dropping of the argument, because it implies how totally they have in fact failed to see each other's point of view. This leads directly into later developments. Sue, with her 'blue-stocking' intellectualism, would certainly not regard the topic as 'hypothetical' and therefore worthless, nor would she in any case regard it as absurd to defend a hypothetical case; her cousin, on the other hand, would object strongly to her unspoken dismissal of the Bible as 'an old book'. We recollect this scene, and it takes on a deeper irony, when much later in the book Sue, torn between her emancipated views and her deep-rooted feelings about marriage, takes refuge, uncharacteristically, in devout church-going.

Much else even in this short passage depends for its richness of nuance and its total effectiveness as a piece of writing on its place in the whole fictional structure – on Jude's pious and narrow but idealistic upbringing in particular, but also on the impressions we have formed of Sue, her innocence, her odd and fascinating mixture of naïveté and worldliness; on the situation both are in when this dialogue takes place, late at night, in Jude's lodgings close to the strict and monastic Training School in Melchester (modelled on Salisbury); and on the way their relationship develops from this point on. There is little we can isolate for critical comment about Hardy's style here. Its chief virtue, as with large portions of any good novel, lies in its 'transparency'. When we read fiction we do not want to be constantly made aware of the language; it does its best work by effacing itself so that nothing comes between us and the author's vision – 'Art lies in concealing art'. This is not to say that close study of passages from fiction will always be useless. We shall be presenting some pieces for study in Part II (e.g. ch. 3, ex. 1; ch. 4, ex. 1A, 7, 17, etc.). But we must always bear in mind that any conclusions we come to are provisional, and may be modified when the passage is seen in the context of the novel as a whole. *Jude the Obscure* contains about 150,000 words; most novels run to at least 80,000 words. In that length we shall almost certainly find sections that are humdrum, merely competent, or even slackly written, just as we shall find highly wrought, intense and poetic passages. To study either kind closely in isolation and to then draw conclusions about the quality of the novel as a whole would be unfair to the novelist.

This does not relieve us of our need to read critically, i.e. with close attention, not necessarily or even primarily to pick faults. Nor does it mean that certain kinds of fictional writing cannot be fairly easily placed and dismissed from serious attention. We do not, for instance, need to sample much of this story to see it for the 'action-packed' thriller that it is, and we are not likely to spend much time reading it closely for its psychological insights into behaviour and motive:

But Rex knew where his duty lay – with the ewe, whose long fleece had caught fast in a thorn bush. Rex was standing beside her, barking his SOS for Mac, and a hundred buffaloes were bearing down upon him. He must have seen them, but he would not leave the ewe.

Mac raced back to him. He whipped out his knife to cut the wool free of the thorns. The buffaloes were almost upon them. Mac had three seconds in which to reach a big grey boulder yards away. Dragging the ewe by one horn and Rex by his collar, he flung himself flat behind the rock and clutched the two to him . . .

Introductions were made. The cowboys grinned sheepishly at Mac. The surly foreman suddenly broke into a grin, too.

'Shake, partner. We were fools mistaking you for a rustler.'

'Say no more, cowboy,' laughed Mac.

We expect stereotypes – 'goodies and baddies' – rather than fully drawn characters, and descriptive passages only when they forward the all-important and 'gripping' story-line. Most of us have read plenty of such stories. They form the printed counterparts of television 'soap operas' and film Westerns – undemanding entertainment for an idle hour. The mistake would be if we assumed that all fiction could be sampled and placed as simply as this.

A note on drama

The study of drama is largely the study of dialogue. A playwright's dialogue is, as we have seen, 'a small visible portion of a gigantic unseen formation'. The writer's choice of words is determined by what he wishes to reveal (or conceal) of this unseen formation. To continue the iceberg image, as in stormy seas giant waves and their following troughs will reveal more of what in calmer waters remains hidden, so will a good dramatist allow the action to work upon hitherto unknown and possibly even unsuspected aspects of the personality he is creating. The bleak sadness of Ophelia's burial, and Laertes' wild speech and wilder actions at the grave-side, force Hamlet into the exaggeration of matching Laertes' leap into the open grave to close with him in unseemly wrangling. The bitterness of the circumstances and, to an even greater extent, Hamlet's own uncontrolled action cause him then to utter words which might well have saved Ophelia's life had she heard them:

Hamlet.   I lov'd Ophelia. Forty thousand brothers
        Could not, with all their quantity of love,
        Make up my sum. What wilt thou do for her?

. . .
Be buried quick with her, and so will I;
And, if thou prate of mountains, let them throw
Millions of acres on us, till our ground,
Singeing his pate against the burning zone,
Make Ossa like a wart.

This one tiny extract from one play, from Shakespeare's massive output, should encourage rather than daunt us. From whatever angle we choose to examine his work its integrity will be apparent. Whether we spend time considering the imagery, the classical references and figures of speech; or the dramatic reasons for their use; or the mood of the speaker at the time and of those around him which may cause him to speak as he does; or yet again the rhythmic properties of the lines and the tempi they suggest for performance – any or all of these areas of study will be valid and rewarding.

When writing plays Shakespeare was a dramatist first and a poet second. When we read *The Family Reunion* by T. S. Eliot we see the poet at work. Eliot is alert to speech rhythms, the following through of poetic images, the effects of symbol and allegory; his words spread themselves, displaying a consciousness of significance. In the second part of the play Agatha and her nephew Harry are speaking of their past lives:

Agatha.   I only looked through the little door
      When the sun was shining on the rose-garden;
      And heard in the distance tiny voices
      And then a black raven flew over.
      And then I was *only my own feet*[4] walking
      Away, down a concrete corridor
      In a dead air. *Only feet* walking
      And sharp heel scraping. *Over and under*.
      Echo and *noise of feet*.
      I was *only the feet, and the eye*

---

[4] Our italics, here and below.

> *Seeing the feet: the unwinking eye*
> Fixing the movement. *Over and under.*
>
> Harry.   In and out, in an endless drift
>   Of shrieking forms in a circular desert
>   Weaving with contagion of putrescent embraces
>   On dissolving bone. *In and out,* the movement
>   *Until the chain broke,* and I was left
>   Under *the single eye* above the desert.
>
> Agatha.   *Up and down,* through the stone passages
>
> . . . .
>   *Up and down. Until the chain breaks.*
> Harry.   *To and fro,* dragging my feet
>
> . . . .
>   . . . . *To and fro.*
>   *Until the chain breaks.*
>   *The chain breaks,*
>   The wheel stops, and the noise of machinery,
>   And the desert is cleared, under the judicial sun
>   *Of the final eye* . . .

The hypnotic repetitions and chanting rhythms have a strong cumulative effect – fantasy and reality side by side, you come to believe it all. Later in this scene Harry says, 'And what did not happen is as true as what did happen.'

In Act Two of *The Caretaker* by Harold Pinter, Aston also talks about his past life:

Aston.   They were all – a good bit older than me. But they always *used to listen.* I thought – they understood what I said. I mean I *used to talk* to them. I talked too much. That was my mistake. The same in the factory. Standing there, or in the breaks, I *used to – talk* about things. And these men, they *used to listen,* whenever I – had anything to say.

Here we also have repetition, which could also be hypnotic. Aston's narrative, which is very long, describes his horror at being treated by E.C.T. in a mental hospital. For Pinter the reality here is sufficient; the many pauses and the repetitions make the narrative dramatically possible. For Eliot the repetitions (he does not indicate a single pause throughout the play) give too much substance to poetic fantasy and thus do away with the need for reality. In *Poetry and Drama*, a lecture delivered at Harvard in 1950, Eliot says of verse drama 'It must justify itself dramatically and not merely be fine poetry shaped into a dramatic form.' The play must be seen before we can decide whether Eliot succeeds in following his own directive. When read, the poetry demands very close attention in its own right. But on a stage, where cardboard and paint, distanced and highlighted, are preferable to marble and gold, where cheap material is as effective as rich brocade and coloured glass takes the place of rubies, plain ordinary words like Aston's can be found to serve their purpose more immediately than Eliot's richer and more esoteric language.

Our ordinary everyday language is limited in its poetic and expressive resources, and writers have had to develop ways of surmounting these limitations in order to create and exploit dramatic situations. Modern playwrights make use of — and playgoers have come to value — silences; implication rather than explanation; understatement and nuance. Our common speech is, as it always has been, the best medium for our best plays. The audiences can fill the silences and pick up the implications with a valid sense of participation because they speak the same language. It is this that makes improvisation possible in the theatre. Athol Fugard's play *Sizwe Bansi is Dead* started as an improvisation. The play is about the South African pass laws. Sizwe Bansi is forced to use the name and pass book of a chance dead man in order to save his own life and protect his family. The play is written in prose, achieving poetic intensity through the simple urgency of the statement, in the mouths of uneducated black labourers. The treatment of the subject-matter has great dramatic power:

Sizwe. Who wants me, friend? What's wrong with me? I'm a man. I've got eyes to see. I've got ears to listen when people talk.

I've got a head to think good things. What's wrong with me?
[He starts to tear off his clothes] Look at me! I'm a man. I've
got legs. I can run with a wheelbarrow full of cement! I'm
strong. I'm a man.

And immediately after this, when his friend Buntu reads
his reference book:

Sizwe.   Buntu, does that book tell you I'm a man? That bloody
   book! . . . People, do you know? No! Wherever you go . . . it's
   that bloody book. You go to school, it goes too. Go to work, it
   goes too. Go to church and pray and sing lovely hymns, it sits
   there with you. Go to hospital and die, it lies there too!

We have noticed the increasing contribution of overseas
writers to English literature. The insight into the life and
hardships of black South Africans we can develop through
reading Fugard's plays has considerable social significance. Moreover the speech rhythms and syntax of the
English spoken by his characters has a vigour and colour
that enriches the language for all who use it.

Writing about reading

Writing about literature, preferably after group dis-
cussions, has two particular advantages. It makes the
reader commit himself, and it makes him see how much
was and always is involved in the act of writing. This
chapter will help you to ask the right questions about a
piece of writing: to what degree is it 'scientific', to what
degree emotive? What is the relative importance of
Sense, Feeling and Tone, and how are they related? What
is the writer's purpose or aim? Does he achieve it? If so,
how, if not, why not? What kind of words does he use,
and is their choice determined by the subject-matter or by
the writer's interpretation of it or manner of dealing with
it? Does that manner include rhythmic effects or imagery?
In the case of an excerpt, do we need to modify our comments or reserve judgment in the light of the original

context of the passage, for example a novel or a play? Finally, what is our own response to the passage, and on what is it based? Can we justify it from evidence drawn from the writing itself? Alternatively, can we appreciate the good qualities of the piece even though we cannot respond to it personally?

Our answers to such questions, suitably arranged and coherently expressed, should form the basis of our critical appreciation. In the rest of this book we present passages for close reading and critical appreciation. For some of them we also set out our responses, or suggest lines of approach. In most cases we believe the writing to be good of its kind – often superlatively good; but a few pieces are included of less worthwhile writing for the sake of comparison. When you have discussed and set out in writing your considered response to a number of these passages we believe that your powers of discrimination in reading will be increased, and your enjoyment of good literature enhanced.

PART II

PRACTICE IN CRITICISM

CHAPTER 3

FIVE PIECES OF WRITING CRITICISED

We have set out in this chapter some critical responses to pieces of prose, poetry and drama. We have said enough in Part I for it to be clear that one person's response to a piece of writing can never be the only 'right' response; it may well be that readers will disagree with some of the opinions here, or that – perhaps in the course of discussion – further insights will be found into the writers' intentions and modes of expression. The criticisms are given partly for this very purpose; partly also to demonstrate the critical principles set out in Chapter Two, and to provide worked examples of the kind of answers expected by examiners in English Literature.

It is our conviction that the work involved in giving close attention to 'the words on the page' can enrich one's understanding and enjoyment of literature.

I

[In this extract from a novel Jack Eccles visits a fellow minister to discuss Harry Angstrom, a parishioner who is also a close friend. Lucy is Jack's wife.]

He gets into the car thirsty and vexed. There was something pleasant said in the last half-hour but he can't remember what it was. He's scratched, hot, confused, and dry; he's spent an afternoon in a bramble patch. He's seen half a dozen people and a dog and nowhere did an opinion tally with his own, that Harry Angstrom was worth saving and could be saved. Instead down there between the brambles there seemed to be no Harry at all: nothing but stale air and last year's dead stalks. Mrs Angstrom's ice water has left him thirstier than before; his palate seems coated with cobwebs. The day is declining through the white afternoon to the long blue spring evening. He drives past a corner where someone is practising on a trumpet behind an open upstairs window. *Du du do do da da dee. Dee dee da da do do du.* Cars are whispering home from work. He drives across the town, tacking on the diagonal streets along a course parallel to the distant ridge of the mountain. Fritz Kruppenbach, Mount Judge's Lutheran minister for twenty-seven years, lives in a high brick house not far from the cemetery. The motor-cycle belonging to his college-age son is on its side in the driveway, partly dismantled. The sloping lawn graded in fussy terraces, has the unnatural chartreuse evenness that comes with much fertilizing, much weed-killing, and much mowing. Mrs Kruppenbach – will Lucy ever achieve that dimpled, obedient look? – comes to the door in a gray dress that makes no compromise with the season. Her gray hair girdles her head with braids of great compactness. When she lets all that hair down, she must be a witch. 'He's mowing out back,' she says.

'I'd like to talk to him for just a few minutes. It's a problem that involves our two congregations.'

'Go up to his room, why do-an tcha? I'll fetch him.'

The house-foyer, halls, staircase, even the minister's leathery den upstairs – is flooded with the smell of beef roasting. As if every day, when the house is cleaned, the odour is rubbed into the wood with a damp rag. Eccles sits by the window of Kruppenbach's den on an oak-backed choir pew left over from some renovation. Seated on the bench he feels an adolescent compulsion to pray but instead peers across the valley at the pale geen fragments of the golf course where he would like to be, with Harry. He lied somewhat to Mrs Angstrom. Harry does not play golf better than he. . . .

In about 400 words comment on the writer's aims, the means used to achieve them, and the total effectiveness of the passage.

The writer's main aim here is to portray the personalities of two obviously very different ministers by describing a meeting between them. It would appear that he is more sympathetic to Eccles, with whom the reader is made to sympathise by being taken inside his consciousness as he experiences the events described here. Eccles is apparently deeply involved, suggesting that Harry is more than a mere parishioner of his.

The passage successfully evokes the Lutheran minister's house, and gives some insight into the characters of both ministers. Our sympathy for Eccles is engaged partly by the method of narration – in the present tense, third person, but giving the effect of first person narrative. The present tense – 'He *gets* into the car', 'He *drives* . . .' etc. – seems at first crude and naïve, but soon becomes acceptable, adding immediacy to the passing events while allowing for momentary flashes of recollection, e.g. 'nowhere *did* an opinion tally', 'He *lied* somewhat . . .' The sense of being inside Jack Eccles, of experiencing his 'stream of consciousness', is heightened by the attention paid to physical, often apparently incongruous, details. We see through his eyes the sloping, too-well-kept lawn and Mrs Kruppenbach's well-groomed hair; we hear the cars 'whispering' home, and the trumpet practice; we even smell the roast beef. These and other details give the effect of a total experience rather than of having been deliberately selected.

Yet when it comes to character delineation the details are seen to be carefully chosen. We have a strong impression of Kruppenbach from his 'high brick house', his obedient wife, his lawns 'in fussy terraces' (he is mowing when Eccles calls), and his 'leathery' den with its oak choir-pew. By contrast, Eccles comes over as sensitive, casual, almost irreverent in manner, but friendly and caring.

The writer uses imagery skilfully. Eccles' fruitless talks on Harry Angstrom's behalf so far are described as 'an afternoon in a bramble patch', and his frustration seems to affect him almost physically – 'scratched, hot, confused, and dry'. Although he has been given iced water he is still thirsty. The solidity of Kruppenbach's house is emphasised by the roast beef smell – 'as if every day, when the house is cleaned, the odour is rubbed into the wood with a damp rag'. Sitting like a petitioner in Kruppenbach's den makes Eccles feel adolescent.

The language is plain, clear and direct, admirably suited to its purpose, neither ornate nor self-conscious.

II

Celia. Alas, sir, be appeased! I could not think
My being at the window should more now
Move your impatience, than at other times.
Corvino. No! not to seek and entertain a parley
With a known knave, before a multitude!
You were an actor with your handkerchief,
Which he most sweetly kist in the receipt,
And might, no doubt, return it with a letter,
And point[1] the place where you might meet; your sister's,
Your mother's, or your aunt's might serve the turn.
Celia. Why, dear sir, when do I make these excuses,
Or ever stir abroad, but to the church?
And that so seldom —
Corvino.   Well, it shall be less;
And thy restraint before was liberty,
To what I now decree: and therefore mark me.
First, I will have this bawdy light[2] damm'd up;
And till't be done, some two or three yards off
I'll chalk a line: o'er which if thou but chance
To set thy desperate foot, more hell, more horror,
More wild remorseless rage shall seize on thee
Than on a conjuror, that had heedless left
His circle's safety ere his devil was laid.
Then here's a lock which I will hang upon thee,
And, now I think on't, I will keep thee backwards;
Thy lodging shall be backwards; thy walks backwards;
Thy prospect, all be backwards; and no pleasure,
That thou shalt know but backwards: nay, since you force

---

[1] appoint.
[2] window.

My honest nature, know, it is your own,
Being too open, makes me use you thus:
Since you will not contain your subtle nostrils
In a sweet room, but they must snuff the air
Of rank and sweaty passengers. [*Knocking within*] — One
 knocks.
Away, and be not seen, pain of thy life;
Nor look toward the window.

Give the gist of this extract from a play, comment on the style, and show how the language serves the writer's dramatic purpose.

Although most of the dialogue is Corvino's the two characters are equally present before the audience, and Celia's reactions to her husband's words would in production be given as much importance as the words themselves. Her half-hearted attempts to placate him, and to counter his extravagant accusations suggest that they are what she has grown accustomed to expect from him: 'Alas, sir, be appeased', 'Why, dear sir . . .' Her two short and rather colourless speeches indicate a protest uttered for form's sake, without strong feeling. In production her words could be made to convey a general attitude and manner — indignant, propitiatory, teasing, tearful, petulant, disdainful — or indeed she could attempt a judicious mixture of several, while keeping a wary eye upon the psychotic manifestations of Corvino's sharp and spiteful nature. We see why when we witness how the most positive assertion of her sense of grievance, her whining 'And that so seldom — ', sparks off Corvino's brutal 'well, it shall be less!' His jealous imagination erupts in virulent, colourful language; he exaggerates the casual sign from the window into 'entertain[ing] a parley', the idle watchers in the street outside into 'a multitude'. He torments himself over the handkerchief episode, his mind's eye already seeing a letter of assignation. He even seems to enjoy this indulgence: there is relish in the venomous antithesis 'And thy restraint before was liberty'. But his need to make it impossible for her to betray him is pathetic in its diseased imaginings; even the window becomes a pander to his wife's lust – 'this bawdy light'. The increase in tempo, the more hectic rhythms of this speech, portray vividly the speed of Corvino's thoughts as he devises ever more fantastic restrictions on Celia's liberty, culminating in the five times repeated 'backwards', the word being placed every time either at a line-ending or on the caesura. After this climax comes a change of tone with his unconsciously ironic claim to an 'honest nature'. The sensual overtones of his tirade become explicit in the reference to Celia's 'subtle nostrils' that are ready to 'snuff the air of rank and sweaty passengers'. Corvino seems to need to ascribe disloyalty and promiscuousness to his wife. In his disordered mind her dropped handkerchief and her occasional excursions become evidence of desperate attempts to deceive him: 'You were an *actor*', 'thy desperate foot'.

The audience would quickly recognise the marks of that stock figure of ridicule the jealous husband with a young wife, towards whom their sympathies would be drawn. The passage, short as it is, gives the actors ample opportunity to develop this almost stereotyped situation in a lively and dramatically convincing manner.

III

Rhapsody on a Windy Night

T. S. Eliot
(see *Collected Poems, 1909–1962* or
Selected Poems, published by Faber)

In 500 to 600 words write an extended appreciation of the poem. State its theme, the means used by the poet to present it, and your own response to the poem as a whole.

The first aim of the poem is to evoke a mood – of loneliness, despair and futility, a resigned fatalism. Normal daylight, and the (deceptive?) orderliness of memory are dissolved, to be replaced by 'a lunar synthesis', to which the regularly placed street-lamps give an arbitrary coherence that emphasises life's triviality. The lamps provide formal links between the five sections, as regular as a clock; yet when they 'speak' they are all one lamp – 'The street-lamp said . . .' 'The lamp hummed . . .', and the slightly artificial diction – 'Regard', 'Remark' etc. – gives the utterances a remote impersonality.

Although the moon is said to 'dissolve the floors of memory' the poem is *about* memory. In the opening section it is totally inconsequential: 'As a madman shakes a dead geranium', an image echoed in section four in the 'reminiscence . . . of sunless dry geraniums' and the moon's paper rose. In section two memory becomes a tide's detritus, and sea images persist in the next section, where two memories are more precisely recalled – the child pocketing a toy, and the old crab. Finally the nocturnal walker is forced by the street-lamp back to full consciousness with the admonitory one-word line 'Memory!' However, he carries the journey and its futilities with him, just as he carries the 'little lamp', whose spreading 'ring on the stair' recalls the stained dress seen earlier.

Every other living thing has intensified the speaker's isolation. The woman, possibly a prostitute, seems sinister and predatory, an impression strengthened by the snarling 'grin' of her door; the cat cowers away, the child had 'nothing' behind its look. The crab was another predator, gripping the stick held out to him.

The images are obsessive. The woman's twisted eye 'like a crooked pin' called up 'a crowd of twisted things', one of which is the brittle and useless spring – a symbol of unused and wasted strength. Images appealing to hearing and smell are equally important: the whispering incantations and the drum, the sputtering, humming gas-lamps, the 'dust and eau de Cologne' and airless female smells – all contribute to the sense of imprisonment when the walker reaches his room.

Throughout the poem rhymes and half-rhymes are used

with cunning, often ironic effect. In section one, for instance, the moon's 'incantations' replace the 'relations', 'divisions' and 'precisions' of daily life, and the 'drum' is made less portentous, more futile, by the strong/weak rhyme with 'geranium'; section four has 'gutter', 'butter' and 'stutters'; in section five we are teased by the string of unsatisfying half-rhymes 'grass', 'face', 'rose', 'corridors', 'bars', and 'geraniums' gets another lop-sided rhyme. The irony of the final command 'prepare for life', emphasised by the tautening of rhythm throughout the section, leads to the inevitability of the strong rhyme life/knife, focusing the 'crowd of twisted things' in a menacing concluding image.

The poem as a whole, by its strongly sensuous evocation of individual isolation and despair, makes a powerful comment on twentieth-century city life.

IV

An Irish Airman Foresees His Death

> I know that I shall meet my fate
> Somewhere among the clouds above;
> Those that I fight I do not hate,
> Those that I guard I do not love;
> My country is Kiltartan Cross,
> My countrymen Kiltartan's poor,
> No likely end could bring them loss
> Or leave them happier than before.
> Nor law, nor duty bade me fight,
> Nor public men, nor cheering crowds,
> A lonely impulse of delight
> Drove to this tumult in the clouds;
> I balanced all, brought all to mind,
> The years to come seemed waste of breath,
> A waste of breath the years behind
> In balance with this life, this death.

Write a critical appreciation of this poem.

The poem is concerned with the airman's premonition of his death and with the intense emotions he experiences as a result. As we read it we become aware that his detachment is not merely the physical isolation of an aviator. He is not motivated by the traditional impulses of fighting men; he neither hates his enemies nor loves his countrymen, and the poor people of his own locality will not be affected by his death. The idea of being a hero does not attract him, nor is he motivated by the conscription law. These ideas are conveyed without the help of colourful or striking images; they would be inappropriate here in the clouds, divorced from the world of the senses. The lines rhyme alternately, and very precisely — there are no half-rhymes. The need for each rhyme as it comes seems inevitable; there is an inescapable movement forward. This is reinforced by the rhythmic impulse, for the most part in a simple iambic pattern. Its regularity gives the trochaic stress on 'Drove' near the climax of the poem greater effect. We are made to feel some of the violence which will mark his last battle in the air.

What prompts the man? Like a mountaineer or a racing driver it is the marvellous yet desperate exhilaration achieved by risking his life purely for the sake of it. Everything becomes centred on one intense moment — the rest of existence is of little importance. The airman tells us he 'balanced all', and indeed the form of the poem conveys an almost physical impression of balancing. The sixteen lines are exactly divided into two sentences. In the first there is measured repetition:

> Those that I fight I do not hate,
> Those that I guard I do not love;

The punctuation also gives a sense of order. Both sentences contain two parts of equal grammatical weight separated by a semi-colon. In the final half-sentence repetition and formal control help the words actually to convey the sense of equilibrium they describe:

> I *balanced all*, brought *all* to mind,
> The *years to come* seemed *waste of breath*,
> A *waste of breath* the *years behind*
> In *balance* with *this* life, *this* death

The sense of the words is obvious, but their position, with 'balanced', 'balance' at the beginning and end of the section, also suggests things poised. This impression is heightened by the neat division of the first of these lines, with four syllables on each side of the comma almost cancelling each other out. In the next two lines the changed word-order, with its see-saw rhythm, has the effect of equating future and past in a strong feeling of negation. The poem ends on a more positive note; the poise achieved has brought to those time-honoured opposites *life* and *death* an equal significance in the airman's dangerous world. If he has lost his joy in living, he has also lost his fear of the unknown.

What emerges finally is an awareness that the airman has successfully reconciled the violent and confused emotions of war with a fatalistic detachment.

Finally in this chapter we give an example of writing with a rather different purpose from the other four. The passage comes from a popular book on astronomy by a physicist, and is followed by one person's strong reaction to it.

V

A

Standing on our microscopic fragment of a grain of sand [the earth], we attempt to discover the nature and purpose of the universe which surrounds our home in space and time. Our first impression is something akin to terror. We find the universe terrifying because of its vast meaningless distances, terrifying because of its inconceivably long vistas of time which dwarf human history to the twinkling of an eye, terrifying because of our extreme loneliness, and because of the material insignificance of our home in space –

a millionth part of a grain of sand out of all the sea-sand in the world. But above all else, we find the universe terrifying because it appears to be indifferent to life like our own; emotion, ambition and achievement, art and religion, all seem equally foreign to its plan. Perhaps indeed we ought to say it appears to be actively hostile to life like our own ...

Into such a universe we have stumbled, if not exactly by mistake, at least as the result of what may properly be described as an accident.

B

Comment   The range and variety of the emotional appeal should be noted – our terror, loneliness and insignificance, the meaningless-ness of distances in the universe, the sentimental associations of 'our home in space and time', 'our home in space', the 'indifference' or even 'hostility' of the universe to us, the pathos of our accidental stumbling into it.

These emotions are fundamentally false. Some can be dismissed at once as such. For instance, hostility or indifference can only characterize a person or at all events a mind. It cannot be predicated of nature unless nature is a person, and at this stage of the argument the author is not postulating any such thing. It is only introduced to terrify the reader. The significance of the 'meaningless distances' is also very obscure. How can any distance have a meaning? And if some distances do have one, how does the author know that those in the universe do not? He might at least have given some sort of indication of the sort of meaning he would expect to find in a distance. The idea of our stumbling into the universe is equally lacking in point. The way in which mankind appeared on the earth does not resemble a stumble more than any other mode of progres-sion. But the word has a helpless and pathetic sound about it and is therefore impressive. 'Extreme loneliness' can also be dismissed quite shortly in view of the fact that loneliness is a psychical rather than a physical state. It is possible for a person to be lonely in a crowded city or not to be lonely on a desert island ...

CHAPTER 4

ANTHOLOGY FOR FURTHER PRACTICE

In this part of the book we provide a wide variety of writing – prose, poetry and drama – for practice in critical appreciation of the kind outlined in Part I and demonstrated in Chapter Three. The authors are not named with the passages, because we believe it is easier to approach a piece of writing honestly if one has as few preconceptions about it as possible. (All the sources are listed on pp. 168–9.) In many instances we have put two passages or poems together. This is not done in order to praise one at the expense of the other, but so that different approaches to similar themes can be studied together.

Some questions relating to particular items are included at the end of the chapter (pp. 165–7). Alternatively, the more general questions used in Chapter Three can be applied to most of the pieces here as well. Students of English literature sometimes find they need more specific critical terms in their written work than are in everyday use. We have added a short glossary of such terms at the end of the book (pp. 173–5).

I

A

'Now try to get higher in this way. You see that tuft of sea-pink above you. Get that well into your hand, but don't trust to it entirely. Then step upon my shoulder, and I think you will reach the top.'

With trembling limbs she did exactly as he told her. The preternatural quiet and solemnity of his manner overspread upon herself, and gave her a courage not her own. She made a spring from the top of his shoulder, and was up.

Then she turned to look at him.

By an ill fate, the force downwards of her bound, added to his own weight, had been too much for the tooth of quartz upon which his feet depended. . . .

It moved. Knight seized a tuft of sea-pink with each hand.

The quartz rock which had been his salvation was worse than useless now. It rolled over, out of sight, and away into the same nether sky that had engulfed the telescope.

One of the tufts by which he held came out at the root, and Knight began to follow the quartz. It was a terrible moment. Elfride uttered a low wild wail of agony, bowed her head, and covered her face with her hands.

Between the turf-covered slope and the gigantic perpendicular rock intervened a weather-worn series of jagged edges, forming a face yet steeper than the former slope. As he slowly slid inch by inch upon these, Knight made a last desperate dash at the lowest tuft of vegetation – the last outlying knot of starved herbage ere the rock appeared in all its bareness. It arrested his further descent. Knight was now literally suspended by his arms; but the incline of the brow being what engineers would call about a third in one, it was sufficient to relieve his arms of a portion of his weight, but was very far from offering an adequately flat face to support him.

In spite of this dreadful tension of body and mind, Knight found time for a moment of thankfulness. Elfride was safe. . . .

[Knowing there was no chance of help before Knight's strength gave out, Elfride used her undergarments to make an emergency rope.]

The rope was now firm in every part.

'When you have let it down,' said Knight, already resuming his position of ruling power, 'go back from the edge of the slope, and over the bank as far as the rope will allow you. Then lean down, and hold the end with both hands.'

He had first thought of a safer plan for his own deliverance, but it involved the disadvantage of possibly endangering her life.

'I have tied it round my waist,' she cried, 'and I will lean directly upon the bank, holding with my hands as well.'

It was the arrangement he had thought of, but would not suggest.

'I will raise and drop it three times when I am behind the bank,' she continued, 'to signify that I am ready. Take care, O, take the greatest care, I beg you!'

She dropped the rope over him, to learn how much of its length it would be necessary to expend on that side of the bank, went back, and disappeared as she had done before.

The rope was trailing by Knight's shoulders. In a few moments it twitched three times.

He waited yet a second or two, then laid hold.

The incline of this upper portion of the precipice, to the length only of a few feet, useless to a climber empty-handed, was invaluable now. Not more than half his weight depended entirely on the linen rope. Half a dozen extensions of the arms, alternating with half a dozen seizures of the rope with his feet, brought him up to the level of the soil.

He was saved, and by Elfride.

He extended his cramped limbs like an awakened sleeper, and sprang over the bank.

At sight of him she leapt to her feet with almost a shriek of joy. Knight's eyes met hers, and with supreme eloquence the glance of each told a long-concealed tale of emotion in that short half-moment. Moved by an impulse neither could resist they ran together and into each other's arms.

B

Sometymes I was in lanes full of rowes of trees and then I came down a very steep stony hill to Louu [Looe], 13 mile, and here I cross'd a little arme of the sea on a bridge of 14 arches; ... Here indeed I met with more inclosed ground and soe had more lanes and a deeper clay road, which by the raine the night before had made it very dirty and full of water; in many places in the road there are many holes and sloughs where with water its difficult to shun danger; here my horse was quite down in one of these holes full of water but by the good hand of God's Providence which had allwayes been with me ever a present help in tyme of need, for giving him a good strap he flounc'd up againe, tho' he had gotten quite down his head and all, yet did retrieve his feete and gott cleer off the place with me on his back.

C

Late on the afternoon of the seventh day Mick Hopkinson's canoe became wedged upside down between two rocks. Repeated attempts to right himself failed. With lungs near to bursting point his canoe broke up around him and he surfaced. Now he was swept rapidly downstream by the current, submerged for much of the time and constantly smashed over rocks, he was helpless and weakening fast. His strength was being sapped away by the ice cold water and to onlookers he was lost as no slack water was visible. For over three-quarters of a mile he was swept along. Mike Jones – barely able to see more than blurred outlines because he was suffering from acute snowblindness – jumped into his canoe and gave chase. Hopkinson twice managed to grasp the back of Jones's boat only to slip back again into the icy waters. The third time he managed to hang on and was dragged half-drowned to the bank. Barely conscious and long past caring, he stumbled up the bank and back to the night's campsite. At this altitude and in water only just above freezing point survival time is only a matter of minutes and Mick Hopkinson was very lucky to be alive. His canoe was lost but the next day he felt sufficiently recovered to carry on canoeing.

Mick – who together with all the canoeists was wearing Damart Double Force underwear – said of his traumatic experience, 'I was very thankful for my Damart underwear which kept me warm enough to avoid losing consciousness completely'.

2

A

Like most singers, he kept them waiting a bit. But at last, just at noon, when the mistress of the house had warranted him to sing, the little feathered exile began as it were to tune his pipes. The savage men gathered round the cage that moment, and amidst the dead stillness the bird uttered some very uncertain chirps, but after a while he seemed to revive his memories, and call his ancient cadences back to him one by one, and string them sotto voce.

And then the same sun that had warmed his little heart at home came glowing down on him here, and he gave music back for it more and more, till at last, amidst breathless silence and glistening eyes of the rough diggers hanging on his voice, out burst in that distant land his English song.

It swelled his little throat and gushed from him with thrilling force and plenty, and every time he checked his song to think of its theme, the green meadows, the quiet stealing streams, the clover he first soared from and the Spring he sang so well, a loud sigh from many a rough bosom, many a wild and wicked heart, told how tight the listeners had held their breath to hear him; and when he swelled with song again, and poured with all his soul the green meadows, the quiet brooks, the honey clover, and the English Spring, the rugged mouths opened and so stayed, and the shaggy lips trembled, and more than one drop trickled from fierce unbridled hearts down bronzed and rugged cheeks. Dulce domum!

B   *Piano*

Softly, in the dusk, a woman is singing to me
Taking me back down the vista of years, till I see
A child sitting under the piano, in the boom of the tingling strings
And pressing the small, poised feet of a mother who smiles as she
    sings.

In spite of myself, the insidious mastery of song
Betrays me back, till the heart of me weeps to belong
To the old Sunday evenings at home, with winter outside
And hymns in the cosy parlour, the tinkling piano our guide.
So now it is vain for the singer to burst into clamour
With the great black piano appassionato. The glamour
Of childish days is upon me, my manhood is cast
Down in the flood of remembrance, I weep like a child for the past.

3

A   *Ode*

We are the music-makers
    And we are the dreamers of dreams,
Wandering by lone sea-breakers,
    And sitting by desolate streams;
World-losers and world-forsakers,

On whom the pale moon gleams:
Yet we are the movers and shakers
Of the world for ever, it seems.

With wonderful deathless ditties
We build up the world's great cities,
And out of a fabulous story
We fashion an empire's glory:
One man with a dream, at pleasure,
Shall go forth and conquer a crown;
And three with a new song's measure
Can trample an empire down.

We, in the ages lying
In the buried past of the earth,
Built Nineveh with our sighing,
And Babel itself with our mirth;
And o'erthrew them with prophesying
To the old of a new world's worth;
For each age is a dream that is dying,
Or one that is coming to birth.

B *What the Chairman Told Tom*

Poetry? It's a hobby.
I run model trains.
Mr. Shaw there breeds pigeons.

It's not work. You don't sweat.
Nobody pays for it.
You *could* advertise soap.

Art, that's opera; or repertory –
The Desert Song.
Nancy was in the chorus.

But to ask for twelve pounds a week –
married, aren't you? –
you've got a nerve.

How could I look a bus conductor
in the face
if I paid you twelve pounds?

Who says it's poetry, anyhow?
My ten year old
can do it *and* rhyme.

I get three thousand and expenses,
a car, vouchers,
but I'm an accountant.

They do what I tell them,
my company.
What do *you* do?

Nasty little words, nasty long words,
it's unhealthy.
I want to wash when I meet a poet.

They're Reds, addicts,
all delinquents.
What you write is rot.

Mr Hines says so, and he's a schoolteacher,
he ought to know.
Go and find *work*.

4

A

[Sir Anthony Absolute has called upon his son Jack, to tell him that he has made over to him a large fortune.]

Jack. Let my future life, sir, speak my gratitude; I cannot express the sense I have of your munificence. – Yet, sir, I presume you would not wish me to quit the army?

Sir A. Oh, that shall be as your wife chooses.

Jack. My wife, sir!

Sir A. Ay, ay, settle that between you – settle that between you.

Jack. A wife, sir, did you say?

Sir A. Ay, a wife – why, did not I mention her before?

Jack. Not a word of her, sir.

Sir A. Odd so! – I mustn't forget her though. – Yes, Jack, the independence I was talking of is by a marriage – the fortune is saddled with a wife – but I suppose that makes no difference.

Jack. Sir! sir! – you amaze me!

Sir A. Why, what the devil's the matter with the fool? Just now you were all gratitude and duty.

Jack. I was, sir, – you talked to me of independence and a fortune, but not a word of a wife.

Sir A. Why – what difference does that make? Odds life, sir! if you have the estate, you must take it with the live stock on it, as it stands. . . .

Jack. Then, sir, I must tell you plainly that my inclinations are fixed on another – my heart is engaged to an angel.

Sir A. Then pray let it send an excuse. It is very sorry – but business prevents its waiting on her.

Jack. But my vows are pledged to her. . . .

Sir A. Hark'ee Jack; – I have heard you for some time with patience – I have been cool – quite cool; but take care – you know I am compliance itself – when I am not thwarted; – no one more easily led – when I have my own way; – but don't put me in a frenzy.

Jack. Sir, I must repeat it – in this I cannot obey you.

Sir A. No damn me! if ever I call you Jack again while I live!

Jack. Nay, sir, but hear me.

Sir A. Sir, I won't hear a word – not a word! not one word! so give me your promise by a nod – and I'll tell you what, Jack – I mean you dog – if you don't, by –

Jack. What, sir, promise to link myself to some mass of ugliness! to –

Sir A. Zounds! sirrah! the lady shall be as ugly as I choose: she shall have a hump on each shoulder; she shall be as crooked as the crescent; her one eye shall roll like the bull's in Cox's Museum; she shall have a skin like a mummy, and the beard of a Jew – she shall be all this, sirrah! – yet I will make you ogle her all day, and sit up all night to write sonnets on her beauty.

B

[Christy Mahon, surrounded by the girls and the Widow Quin, is telling them of his father's plans for him to marry.]

Christy (shy but flattered). We were digging spuds in his cold, sloping, stony, divil's patch of a field.

Widow Quin. And you went asking money of him, or making talk of getting a wife would drive him from his farm?

Christy. I did not, then; but there I was, digging and digging, and 'You squinting idiot', says he, 'let you walk down now and tell the priest you'll wed the Widow Casey in a score of days.'

Widow Quin. And what kind was she?

Christy (with horror). A walking terror from beyond the hills, and she two score and five years, and two hundredweights and five pounds in the weighing scales, with a limping leg on her, and a blinded eye, and she a woman of noted misbehaviour with the old and young.

Girls (clustering round him, serving him). Glory be.

Widow Quin. And what did he want driving you to wed with her?

Christy. He was letting on I was wanting a protector from the harshness of the world, and he without a thought the whole while but how he'd have her hut to live in and her gold to drink.

Widow Quin. There's maybe worse than a dry hearth and a widow woman and your glass at night. So you hit him then?

Christy (getting almost excited). I did not. 'I won't wed her,' says I, 'when all know she did suckle me for six weeks when I came into the world, and she a hag this day with a tongue on her has the crows and seabirds scattered, the way they wouldn't cast a shadow on her garden with the dread of her curse.'

Widow Quin (teasingly). That one should be right company.

Sara (eagerly). Don't mind her. Did you kill him then?

Christy. 'She's too good for the like of you,' says he, 'and go on now or I'll flatten you out like a crawling beast has passed under a dray.' 'You will not if I can help it,' says I. 'Go on,' says he, 'or I'll have the divil making garters of your limbs to-night.' 'You will not if I can help it,' says I.

He sits up brandishing his mug.

Sara.   You were right surely.

Christy (impressively).   With that the sun came out between the cloud and the hill, and it shining green in my face. 'God have mercy on your soul,' says he, lifting a scythe. 'Or on your own,' says I, raising the loy.

Susan.   That's a grand story.

Honor.   He tells it lovely.

Christy (flattered and confident).   He gave a drive with the scythe, and I gave a lep to the east. Then I turned around with my back to the north, and I hit a blow on the ridge of his skull, laid him stretched out, and he split to the knob of his gullet.

Girls (together).   Well, you're a marvel! Oh, God bless you! You're the lad, surely!

5

A *The Piano Tuner*

Every six months his white stick brings him,
Punctilious to the minim stroke of nine
On the day we dread. Edgy at his knock,
We infuse a grudging warmth into voices
Asking his health, attempt to ease his coat
From him, which courtesy he refuses;

And usher him to the instrument. He entrusts
Us with nothing, disdains, from his black tent,
Our extended hands where the awkward staircase
Bends, rattles the banisters with his bag,
Crabs past the chairs. Finally at the keyboard
He discharges quick arpeggios of judgement.

'As I expected,' he says, dismissing us;
And before we close the door excludes us
Further, intent in his flummox of strange tools
And a language beyond us. He begins to adjust
And insist on the quotients and ratios
Of order in encased reverberant wire.

93

All morning, then, downstairs we cower;
The thin thunder of decibels, octaves slowly
Made absolute, which will not break into storm,
Dividing us from him. The house is not the same
Until long after he leaves, having made one thing
Perfect. 'Now play,' say his starched eyes.

B   *Thatcher*

Bespoke for weeks, he turned up some morning
Unexpectedly, his bicycle slung
With a light ladder and a bag of knives.
He eyed the old rigging, poked at the eaves,

Opened and handled sheaves of lashed wheat-straw.
Next, the bundled rods: hazel and willow
Were flicked for weight, twisted in case they'd snap.
It seemed he spent the morning warming up:

Then fixed the ladder, laid out well honed blades
And snipped at straw and sharpened ends of rods
That, bent in two, made a white-pronged staple
For pinning down his world, handful by handful.

Couchant for days on sods above the rafters
He shaved and flushed the butts, stitched all together
Into a sloped honeycomb, a stubble patch,
And left them gaping at his Midas touch.

6

A   *An Epistle to Master Arthur Squib*

What I am not, and what I faine would be,
    Whilst I informe my selfe, I would teach thee,
My gentle Arthur; that it might be said
    One lesson we have both learn'd, and well read;
I neither am, nor art thou one of those

That hearkens to a Jacks-pulse, when it goes.
Nor ever trusted to that friendship yet,
  Was issue of the Taverne, or the Spit:
Much lesse a name would we bring up, or nurse,
  That could but claime a kindred from the purse.
Those are poore Ties, depend on those false ends,
  'Tis vertue alone, or nothing, that knits friends:
And as within your Office, you doe take
  No piece of money, but you know, or make
Inquirie of the worth: So must we doe,
  First weigh a friend, then touch, and trie him too:
For there are many slips, and Counterfeits.
  Deceit is fruitfull. Men have Masques and nets,
But these with wearing will themselves unfold:
  They cannot last. No lie grew ever old.
Turne him, and see his Threds: looke, if he be
  Friend to himselfe, that would be friend to thee.
For that is first requir'd, A man be his owne.
  But he that's too-much that, is friend of none.
Then rest, and a friends value understand,
  It is a richer Purchase than of land.

B
[Everyman, summoned by Death to make his reckoning, casts about him for companions to go with him.]

Everyman.   I shall show you how it is;
    Commanded I am to go a journey,
    A long way, hard and dangerous,
    And give a strait count without delay
    Before the high judge Adonai.
    Wherefore I pray you, bear me company,
    As ye have promised, in this journey.
Fellowship.   That is matter indeed! Promise is duty,
    But, and I should take such a voyage on me,
    I know it well, it should be to my pain:
    Also it make me afeard, certain.

95

But let us take counsel here as well as we can,
For your words would fear a strong man.

Everyman.   Why, ye said, If I had need,
Ye would me never forsake, quick nor dead,
Though it were to hell truly.

Fellowship.   So I said, certainly,
But such pleasures be set aside, thee sooth to say:
And also, if we took such a journey,
When should we come again?

Everyman.   Nay, never again till the day of doom.

Fellowship.   In faith, then will not I come there!
Who hath you these tidings brought?

Everyman.   Indeed, *Death* was with me here.

Fellowship.   Now, by God that all hath bought,
If *Death* were the messenger,
For no man that is living to-day
I will not go that loath journey –
Not for the father that begat me!

Everyman.   Ye promised other wise, pardie.

Fellowship.   I wot well I say so truly;
And yet if thou wilt eat, and drink, and make good cheer,
Or haunt to women, the lusty company,
I would not forsake you, while the day is clear,
Trust me verily!

Everyman.   Yea, thereto ye would be ready;
To go to mirth, solace, and play
Your mind will sooner apply
Than to bear me company in my long journey.

Fellowship.   Now, in good faith, I will not that way.
But and thou wilt murder, or any man kill,
In that I will help thee with a good will!

Everyman.   O that is a simple advice indeed!
Gentle *fellow*, help me in my necessity;
We have loved long, and now I need,
And now, gentle *Fellowship*, remember me.

Fellowship.   Whether ye have loved me or no,
By Saint John, I will not with thee go.

Everyman.   Yet I pray thee, take the labour, and do so much for me

To bring me forward, for saint charity,
And comfort me till I come without the town.
Fellowship.   Nay, and thou would give me a new gown,
    I will not with thee go;
    But and you had tarried I would not have left thee so.
    And as now, God speed thee in thy journey,
    For from thee I will depart as fast as I may.
Everyman.   Whither away, *Fellowship?* will you forsake me?
Fellowship.   Yea, by my fay, to God I betake thee.
Everyman.   Farewell, good *Fellowship?* for this my heart is sore;
    Adieu for ever, I shall see thee no more.
Fellowship.   In faith, *Everyman,* farewell now at the end;
    For you I will remember that parting is mourning.
Everyman.   Alack! shall we thus depart indeed?
    Our Lady, help, without any more comfort,
    Lo, *Fellowship* forsaketh me in my most need:
    For help in this world whither shall I resort?
    Fellowship herebefore with me would merry make;
    And now little sorrow for me doth he take.
    It is said, in prosperity men friends may find,
    Which in adversity be full unkind.
    Now whither for succour shall I flee,
    Sith that *Fellowship* hath forsaken me?

7

. . . Captain Marpole's grizzled head emerged from the scuttle.
A sea-dog: clear blue eyes of a translucent trustworthiness: a merry,
wrinkled, morocco-coloured face: a rumbling voice.

'He's too good to be true,' whispered Mrs. Thornton.

'Not at all! It's a sophism to imagine people don't conform to
type!' barked Mr. Thornton. He felt at sixes and sevens.

Captain Marpole certainly looked the ideal Children's Captain.
He would, Mrs. Thornton decided, be careful without being fussy —
for she was all in favour of courageous gymnastics, though glad she
would not have to witness them herself. Captain Marpole cast his
eyes benignantly over the swarming imps.

'They'll worship him,' she whispered to her husband. (She meant, of course, that he would worship them.) It was an important point, this, of the captain: important as the personality of a headmaster.

'So that's the nursery, eh?' said the captain, crushing Mrs. Thornton's hand. She strove to answer, but found her throat undoubtedly paralysed. Even Mr. Thornton's ready tongue was at a loss. He looked hard at the captain, jerked his thumb towards the children, wrestled in his mind with an elaborate speech, and finally enunciated in a small, unlikely voice:

'Smack 'em.'

Then the captain had to go about his duties: and for an hour the father and mother sat disconsolately on the main hatch, quite deserted. Even when all was ready for departure it was impossible to muster the flock for a collective good-bye.

8

[Simon Eyre, the shoemaker, recently made Master Sheriff, is with his wife dining by invitation with the Lord Mayor at Old Ford.]

Lord Mayor. Trust me, you are welcome to Old Ford
    As I myself.
Margery. Truly, I thank your lordship.
Lord Mayor. Would our bad cheer were worth the thanks
    you give.
Eyre. Good cheer, my lord mayor, fine cheer! A fine house, fine walls, all fine and neat.
Lord Mayor. Now, by my troth, I'll tell thee, Master Eyre,
    It does me good, and all my brethren,
    That such a madcap fellow as thyself
    Is entered into our society.
Margery. Ay, but, my lord, he must learn now to put on gravity.
Eyre. Peace, Maggy, a fig for gravity! When I go to Guildhall in my scarlet gown, I'll look as demurely as a saint, and speak as gravely as a justice of peace; but now I am here at Old Ford, at my good Lord Mayor's house, let it go by, vanish, Maggy, I'll be

merry; away with flip-flap, these fooleries, these gulleries. What, honey? Prince am I none, yet am I princely born. What says my lord mayor?

Lord Mayor. Ha, ha, ha! I had rather than a thousand pound, I had an heart but half so light as yours.

Eyre. Why, what should I do, my lord? A pound of care pays not a dream of debt. Hum, let's be merry, whiles we are young; old age, sack and sugar will steal upon us, ere we be aware.

Lord Mayor. It's well done; Mistress Eyre, pray, give good counsel
To my daughter.

Margery. I hope, Mistress Rose will have the grace to take nothing that's bad.

Lord Mayor. Pray God she do; for i' faith, Mistress Eyre,
I would bestow upon that peevish girl
A thousand marks more than I mean to give her
Upon condition she'd be ruled by me.
The ape still crosseth me. There came of late
A proper gentleman of fair revenues
Whom gladly I would call [a] son-in-law:
But my fine cockney would have none of him.
You'll prove a coxcomb for it, ere you die:
A courtier, or no man must please your eye.

Eyre. Be ruled, sweet Rose: th'art ripe for a man. Marry not with a boy that has no more hair on his face than thou hast on thy cheeks. A courtier? wash, go by! stand not upon pishery-pashery: those silken fellows are but painted images, outsides, outsides, Rose; their inner linings are torn. No, my fine mouse, marry me with a gentleman grocer like my lord mayor, your father; a grocer is a sweet trade: plums, plums. Had I a son or daughter should marry out of the generation and blood of the shoemakers, he should pack; what, the Gentle Trade is a living for a man through Europe, through the world.

9

A

Men Improve With the Years

I am worn out with dreams;
A weather-worn, marble triton
Among the streams;
And all day long I look
Upon this lady's beauty
As though I had found in book
A pictured beauty,
Pleased to have filled the eyes
Or the discerning ears,
Delighted to be but wise,
For men improve with the years;
And yet, and yet,
Is this my dream, or the truth?
O would that we had met
When I had my burning youth!
But I grow old among dreams,
A weather-worn, marble triton
Among the streams.

B

The Self-Unseeing

Here is the ancient floor,
Footworn and hollowed and thin,
Here was the former door
Where the dead feet walked in.

She sat here in her chair,
Smiling into the fire;
He who played stood there,
Bowing it higher and higher.

Childlike, I danced in a dream;
Blessings emblazoned that day;
Everything glowed with a gleam;
Yet we were looking away!

10

Factory Worker

walks down each his separate tunnel
past the grey flowers of neighbours'
gardens and last night's parties still
hanging like a bat in ochre caves
smelling of must and urine:
                to where
self must be coagulated, churned
by the pulverizing synthetic lights
and the syren take its toll of dreamers
at each grey tunnel end, delivering
with a glanced valediction at the sportspage
husband
   father
      emperor
of the grey silences, packaged
to the notating ivory gates,
         and behind him,
as the day's portcullis drops
and the sun through dirty glass
coughs sarcastically behind him
as the first joke of the day passes
the first time round – now behind him
where his children wake and frost the air to school
some centuries behind, the grass is green.

11

A

Shall I compare thee to a summer's day?
Thou art more lovely and more temperate.
Rough winds do shake the darling buds of May,
And summer's lease hath all too short a date:
Sometime too hot the eye of heaven shines,

And often is his gold complexion dimm'd;
And every fair from fair some time declines,
By chance, or nature's changing course, untrimm'd;
But thy eternal summer shall not fade
Nor lose possession of that fair thou ow'st;
Nor shall Death brag thou wand'rest in his shade,
When in eternal lines to time thou grow'st.
So long as men can breathe or eyes can see,
So long lives this, and this gives life to thee.

B   *Forever And a Day*

Love like ours was meant to last for ever,
Nothing could destroy our dream divine,
That is why I say that I could never ever
Live without you, dear. You are mine, darling.

I shall always love you,
I'll be thinking of you
Forever and a Day.
I shall still remember
Moments that were tender
Forever and a Day.
How could I forget we made a promise,
We'd be true in rain or in shine.
Love will last for ever,
Ours we'll share together
Forever and a Day.

I 2

[Shylock attempts to justify his insistence on claiming his due, a pound of Antonio's flesh.]

Shylock.   Some men there are love not a gaping pig;
        Some that are mad if they behold a cat;
        And others, when the bagpipe sings i' th' nose,

    Cannot contain their urine; for affection,
    Mistress of passion, sways it to the mood
    Of what it likes or loathes. Now, for your answer:
    As there is no firm reason to be rend'red
    Why he cannot abide a gaping pig;
    Why he, a harmless necessary cat;
    Why he, a woollen bagpipe, but of force
    Must yield to such inevitable shame
    As to offend, himself being offended;
    So can I give no reason, nor I will not,
    More than a lodg'd hate and a certain loathing
    I bear Antonio, that I follow thus
    A losing suit against him. Are you answered?

Bassanio.   This is no answer, thou unfeeling man,
    To excuse the current of thy cruelty.

Shylock.   I am not bound to please thee with my answers.

Bassanio.   Do all men kill the things they do not love?

Shylock.   Hates any man the thing he would not kill?

Bassanio.   Every offence is not a hate at first.

Shylock.   What, wouldst thou have a serpent sting thee twice?

Antonio.   I pray you, think you question with the Jew . . .
    You may as well use question with the wolf,
    Why he hath made the ewe bleat for the lamb;
    You may as well forbid the mountain pines
    To wag their high tops and to make no noise
    When they are fretten with the gusts of heaven;
    You may as well do any thing most hard
    As seek to soften that – than which what's harder? –
    His Jewish heart. Therefore, I do beseech you,
    Make no more offers, use no farther means,
    But with all brief and plain conveniency
    Let me have judgment, and the Jew his will.

Bassanio.   For thy three thousand ducats here is six.

Shylock.   If every ducat in six thousand ducats
    Were in six parts, and every part a ducat,
    I would not draw them; I would have my bond.

Duke.   How shalt thou hope for mercy, rend'ring none?

Shylock.   What judgment shall I dread, doing no wrong?

13

But lo from forth a copse that neighbours by,
A breeding jennet, lusty, young and proud,
Adonis' trampling courser doth espy,
And forth she rushes, snorts and neighs aloud:
   The strong-neck'd steed being tied unto a tree,
   Breaketh his rein, and to her straight goes he.

Imperiously he leaps, he neighs, he bounds,
And now his woven girths he breaks asunder;
The bearing earth with his hard hoof he wounds,
Whose hollow womb resounds like heaven's thunder;
   The iron bit he crusheth 'tween his teeth,
   Controlling what he was controlled with.

His ears up-prick'd, his braided hanging mane
Upon his compass'd crest now stand on end;
His nostrils drink the air, and forth again
As from a furnace, vapours doth he send;
   His eye which scornfully glisters like fire
   Shows his hot courage and his high desire.

Sometime he trots, as if he told the steps,
With gentle majesty and modest pride;
Anon he rears upright, curvets and leaps,
As who should say 'Lo thus my strength is tried:
   And this I do to captivate the eye
   Of the fair breeder that is standing by.'

What recketh he his rider's angry stir,
His flattering 'holla' or his 'Stand, I say'?
What cares he now for curb or pricking spur,
For rich caparisons or trappings gay?
   He sees his love, and nothing else he sees,
   For nothing else with his proud sight agrees.

Look when a painter would surpass the life
In limning out a well-proportion'd steed,

His art with nature's workmanship at strife,
As if the dead the living should exceed:
   So did this horse excel a common one,
   In shape, in courage, colour, pace and bone.

Round-hoof'd, short-jointed, fetlocks shag and long,
Broad breast, full eye, small head, and nostril wide,
High crest, short ears, straight legs and passing strong,
Thin mane, thick tail, broad buttock, tender hide:
   Look what a horse should have he did not lack,
   Save a proud rider on so proud a back.

Sometime he scuds far off, and there he stares;
Anon he starts at stirring of a feather.
To bid the wind a base he now prepares,
And where he run or fly, they know not whether,
   For through his mane and tail the high wind sings,
   Fanning the hairs, who wave like feather'd wings.

He looks upon his love, and neighs unto her:
She answers him, as if she knew his mind.
Being proud, as females are, to see him woo her,
She puts on outward strangeness, seems unkind,
   Spurns at his love, and scorns the heat he feels,
   Beating his kind embracements with her heels.

Then like a melancholy malcontent,
He vails his tail that like a falling plume
Cool shadow to his melting buttock lent;
He stamps, and bites the poor flies in his fume.
   His love perceiving how he was enrag'd,
   Grew kinder, and his fury was assuag'd.

14

Solar Radiation

It is difficult to appreciate what a temperature of 20,000,000° C.
means. If the solar surface and not the centre were as hot as this,
the radiation emitted into space would be so great that the whole

Earth would be vaporized within a few minutes. Indeed, this is just what would happen if some cosmic giant were to peel off the outer layers of the Sun like skinning an orange, for the tremendously hot inner regions would then be exposed. Fortunately, no such circumstance is possible, and the outer layers of the Sun provide a sort of blanket that protects us from its inner fires. Yet in spite of these blanketing layers some energy must leak through from the Sun's centre to its outer regions, and this leakage is of just the right amount to compensate for the radiation emitted by the surface into surrounding space. For if the amount leaking through were greater than the amount radiated, the surface would simply warm up until an exact balance was reached. The situation has some similarities with what happens if you heat a long metal bar at one end. Heat travels from the hotter end to the cooler end. But this analogy is not perfect. Analogies never are. Heat is carried along a metal bar by conduction, whereas in the Sun the outward leak of energy is carried by radiation. The radiation changes its character as it works its way outwards. At the surface it is ordinary light and heat, but in the central regions it takes the form of the very short wavelength radiation known as X-rays.

15

A

After tea Kezia wandered back to their own house. Slowly she walked up the back steps, and through the scullery into the kitchen. Nothing was left in it but a lump of gritty yellow soap in one corner of the kitchen window-sill and a piece of flannel stained by a blue-bag in another. The fire-place was choked up with rubbish. She poked among it but found nothing except a hair-tidy with a heart painted on it that had belonged to the servant girl. Even that she left lying and she trailed through the narrow passage into the drawing-room. The Venetian blind was pulled down but not drawn close. Long pencil rays of sunlight shone through and the wavy shadow of a bush outside danced on the gold lines. Now it was still, now it began to flutter again, and now it came almost as far as her feet. Zoom! Zoom! a blue-bottle knocked against the ceiling; the carpet tacks had little bits of red fluff sticking to them.

B

The grainy sand had gone from under his feet. His boots trod again a damp crackling mast, razor-shells creaking pebbles, that on the un-numbered pebbles beat, woods sieved by the shipworm, lost Armada. Unwholesome sandflats waited to suck his treading soles, breathing upward sewage breath. He coasted them, walking warily. A porter-bottle stood up, stogged to its waist, in the cakey sand dough. A sentinel: isle of dreadful thirst. Broken hoops on the shore; at the land a maze of dark cunning nets; further away chalk-scrawled back-doors and on the higher beach a drying-line with two crucified shirts.

16

Filling Station

Oh, but it is dirty!
– this little filling station,
oil-soaked, oil-permeated
to a disturbing, over-all
black translucency.
Be careful with that match!

Father wears a dirty,
oil-soaked monkey suit
that cuts him under the arms,
and several quick and saucy
and greasy sons assist him
(it's a family filling station),
all quite thoroughly dirty.

Do they live in the station?
It has a cement porch
behind the pumps, and on it
a set of crushed and grease-
impregnated wickerwork;
on the wicker sofa
a dirty dog, quite comfy.

Some comic books provide
the only note of colour –
of certain colour. They lie
upon a big dim doily
draping a taboret
(part of the set), beside
a big hirsute begonia.

Why the extraneous plant?
Why the taboret?
Why, oh why, the doily?
(Embroidered in daisy stitch
with marguerites, I think,
and heavy with gray crochet.)

Somebody embroidered the doily.
Somebody waters the plant,
or oils it, maybe. Somebody
arranges the rows of cans
so that they softly say:
ESSO-SO-SO-SO
to high-strung automobiles.
Somebody loves us all.

17

A

. . . It was an instinctive gesture that made him reach then for the
bainin of Uncle James. He felt it bunched in his hand and he held
on to it. He even reached his other hand and grabbed it with that too
– the dying grip of the drowning man – and then he felt something
under his feet. Rocks? The bottom of the sea? The boat? But it was
firm and he stood on it and he stood straight, and to his cold surprise
he felt air around his head and he hauled on the bainin and Uncle
James was in his hands, a tired heavy weight, and then the feet were
swept from under him again and he felt the water pouring into his
lungs, and then it seemed that he was caught by hands and raised
into the air and his body thumped down on black slimy things that
must be rocks. He freed an arm and grasped with it. It closed round

seaweed. He pulled with the other. The soused white bainin with Uncle James came up beside him. He felt the water pouring over him again, and he dug in his hand and he rode the rock with his knees as if he was on a horse, and he was ready when the sea went back sucking, and he pulled himself up more, and then with an effort which he would never again in this life be able to emulate he stood up on that rock, and he pulled the limp body of his uncle up with him, and he took a step and he took two steps and then he fell, holding tight to the coat, and he felt rough sand on his face like the cloth of a tweed coat, and he pushed with his knees and got to them and he was hunched like that when the water broke over him again thundering, and he took it on his bowed back and when it retreated, still sucking, he got to his feet again, but he couldn't pull any more at his uncle. He walked forward and he dragged him behind him, and he walked four paces and he fell again, and it was still sand and the sea washed over him, but it seemed to have lost its power, so he rested there awhile and then he rose again and he went on again and he kept going on.

B

. . . . He sank down, saw without comprehension that the green water was no longer empty. There was yellow and brown. He heard not the formless mad talking of uncontrolled water but a sudden roar. Then he went under into a singing world and there were hairy shapes that flitted and twisted past his face, there were sudden notable details close to of intricate rock and weed. Brown tendrils slashed across his face, then with a destroying shock he hit solidity. It was utter difference, it was under his body, against his knees and face, he could close fingers on it, for an instant he could even hold on. His mouth was needlessly open and his eyes so that he had a moment of close and intent communion with three limpets, two small and one large that were only an inch or two from his face. Yet this solidity was terrible and apocalyptic after the world of inconstant wetness. It was not vibrant as a ship's hull might be but merciless and mother of panic. It had no business to interrupt the thousands of miles of water going about their purposeless affairs and therefore the world sprang here into sudden war. He felt himself picked up and away from the limpets, reversed, tugged, thrust down into weed and darkness. Ropes held him, slipped and let him go. He saw light, got a mouthful of air and foam. He glimpsed a riven rock face with trees of spray growing up it and the sight of this rock floating in mid-Atlantic was so dreadful that he wasted his air by screaming as if it had been a wild beast. He went under into a green calm, then up and was thrust sideways. The sea no longer played with him. It stayed its wild movement and held him gently, carried him with delicate and careful motion like a retriever with a bird. Hard things touched him about the feet and knees. The sea laid him down gently and retreated. There were hard things touching his face and chest, the side of his forehead. The sea came back and fawned round his face, licked him. He thought movements that did not happen. The sea came back and he thought the movements again and this time they happened because the sea took most of his weight. They moved him forward over the hard things. Each wave and each movement moved him forward. He felt the sea run down to smell at his feet then come back and nuzzle under his arm. It no longer licked his face. There was a pattern in front of him that occupied all the space under the arches. It meant nothing. The sea nuzzled under his arm again.

He lay still.

18

A

[Samuel Plimsoll published a pamphlet *Our Seamen* in 1873 as part of his campaign against the practice of sending rotten, over-loaded and over-insured ships to sea. After citing a number of cases in which ships had sunk almost as soon as they had sailed, he went on:]

Do you doubt these statements? Then, for God's sake – oh, for God's sake, help me to get a Royal Commission to inquire into their truth! Surely I don't ask too much, in asking that, for the sake of these poor brothers of ours, so shamefully neglected, so murderously treated . . .

Working men, is it nothing to you that your fellow-workmen, fathers of families, men to whom life is as dear as it is to yourselves, men who have committed no fault, should thus shamefully be neglected? – should thus be drowned by the dozen and the score to make a few bad men richer? – and that their needless deaths should not even elicit an inquiry into the cause of it? I hate to appeal to class feelings or prejudices, but class jealousy can only be allayed by justice, not by ignoring murderous wrong; and I ask, seriously and sadly, can anyone doubt, but that if these brave men had been pigs or sheep, the legislature had long since been compelled by powerful advocates to stop such losses. Pigs and sheep are property, and property is well represented in Parliament; but these – why they are only our poor brothers, and no one speaks for them.

B

By this means our liberty becomes a noble freedom. It carries an imposing and majestic aspect. It has a pedigree and illustrious ancestors. It has its bearings and its ensigns armorial. It has its gallery of portraits; its monumental inscriptions; its records, evidences, and titles. We procure reverence to our civil institutions on the principle upon which nature teaches us to revere individual men; on account of their age; and on account of those from whom they are descended. All your sophisters cannot produce any thing better adapted to preserve a rational and manly freedom than the course that we have pursued, who have chosen our nature rather than our speculations, our breasts rather than our inventions, for the great conservatories and magazines of our rights and privileges.

(*sophister*, a subtle arguer; *magazine*, store-house)

19

Binsey Poplars

A

My aspens dear, whose airy cages quelled,
Quelled or quenched in leaves the leaping sun,
All felled, felled, are all felled;
   Of a fresh and following folded rank
     Not spared, not one
     That dandled a sandalled
    Shadow that swam or sank
On meadow and river and wind-wandering
    weed-winding bank.

O if we but knew what we do
    When we delve or hew –
Hack and rack the growing green!
    Since country is so tender
To touch, her being so slender,
That, like this sleek and seeing ball
But a prick will make no eye at all,
Where we, even where we mean
    To mend her we end her,
    When we hew or delve:
After-comers cannot guess the beauty been.
    Ten or twelve, only ten or twelve
        Strokes of havoc unselve
            The sweet especial scene,
        Rural scene, a rural scene,
Sweet especial rural scene.

B   *Reservoirs*

There are places in Wales I don't go:
Reservoirs that are the subconscious
Of a people, troubled far down
With gravestones, chapels, villages even;
The serenity of their expression
Revolts me, it is a pose
For strangers, a watercolour's appeal
To the mass, instead of the poem's
Harsher conditions. There are the hills,
Too; gardens gone under the scum
Of the forests; and the smashed faces
Of the farms with the stone trickle
Of their tears down the hills' side.

Where can I go, then, from the smell
Of decay, from the putrefying of a dead
Nation? I have walked the shore
For an hour and seen the English
Scavenging among the remains

Of our culture, covering the sand
Like the tide and, with the roughness
Of the tide, elbowing our language
Into the grave that we have dug for it.

20

[The Duchess, imprisoned, and surrounded by madmen by her brother Ferdinand, is visited shortly before her murder by Bosola in the guise of an old man.]

Duchess. Thou art not mad, sure: dost know me?

Bosola. Yes.

Duchess. Who am I?

Bosola. Thou art a box of worm-seed, at best but a salvatory of green mummy. What's this flesh? a little crudded milk, fantastical puff-paste. Our bodies are weaker than those paperprisons boys used to keep flies in; more contemptible, since ours is to preserve earthworms. Didst thou ever see a lark in a cage? Such is the soul in the body: this world is like her little turf of grass, and the heaven o'er our heads, like her looking-glass, only gives us a miserable knowledge of the small compass of our prison.

Duchess. Am not I thy duchess?

Bosola. Thou art some great woman, sure, for riot begins to sit on thy forehead (clad in grey hairs) twenty years sooner than on a merry milkmaid's. Thou sleep'st worse than if a mouse should be forc'd to take up her lodging in a cat's ear: a little infant that breeds its teeth, should it like with thee, would cry out, as if thou wert the more unquiet bedfellow.

Duchess. I am Duchess of Malfi still.

Bosola. That makes thy sleeps so broken:
Glories, like glow-worms, afar off shine bright,
But looked to near, have neither heat nor light.

Duchess. Thou art very plain.

Bosola. My trade is to flatter the dead, not the living; I am a tomb-maker.

Duchess. And thou com'st to make my tomb?

Bosola. Yes.

Duchess. Let me be a little merry: — of what stuff will you make it?

Bosola. Nay, resolve me first, of what fashion?

Duchess. Why, do we grow fantastical in our death-bed? do we affect fashion in the grave?

Bosola. Most ambitiously. Princes' images on their tombs do not lie, as they were wont, seeming to pray up to heaven; but with their hands under their cheeks, as if they died of the toothache: they are not carved with their eyes fix'd upon the stars; but as their minds were wholly bent upon the world, the self-same way they seem to turn their faces.

21

Mr Bleaney

'This was Mr Bleaney's room. He stayed
The whole time he was at the Bodies, till
They moved him.' Flowered curtains, thin and frayed,
Fall to within five inches of the sill,

Whose window shows a strip of building land,
Tussocky, littered. 'Mr Bleaney took
My bit of garden properly in hand.'
Bed, upright chair, sixty-watt bulb, no hook

Behind the door, no room for books or bags —
'I'll take it.' So it happens that I lie
Where Mr Bleaney lay, and stub my fags
On the same saucer-souvenir, and try

Stuffing my ears with cotton-wool, to drown
The jabbering set he egged her on to buy.
I know his habits — what time he came down,
His preference for sauce to gravy, why

He kept on plugging at the four aways —
Likewise their yearly frame: the Frinton folk
Who put him up for summer holidays,
And Christmas at his sister's house in Stoke.

But if he stood and watched the frigid wind
Tousling the clouds, lay on the fusty bed
Telling himself that this was home, and grinned,
And shivered, without shaking off the dread

That how we live measures our own nature,
And at his age having no more to show
Than one hired box should make him pretty sure
He warranted no better, I don't know.

22

Fear no more the heat o' th' sun
Nor the furious winter's rages;
Thou thy worldly task hast done,
Home art gone, and ta'en thy wages.
Golden lads and girls all must,
As chimney-sweepers, come to dust.

Fear no more the frown o' th' great;
Thou art past the tyrant's stroke.
Care no more to clothe and eat;
To thee the reed is as the oak.
The sceptre, learning, physic, must
All follow this and come to dust.

Fear no more the lightning flash,
Nor th' all-dreaded thunder-stone;
Fear not slander, censure rash;
Thou hast finish'd joy and moan.
All lovers young, all lovers must
Consign to thee and come to dust.

No exorciser harm thee!
Nor no witchcraft charm thee!
Ghost unlaid forbear thee!
Nothing ill come near thee!
Quiet consummation have,
And renowned be thy grave!

23

A

. . . They gradually ascended for half a mile, and then found themselves at the top of a considerable eminence, where the wood ceased, and the eye was instantly caught by Pemberley House, situated on the opposite side of a valley, into which the road with some abruptness wound. It was a large, handsome, stone building, standing well on rising ground, and backed by a ridge of high woody hills; – and in front, a stream of some natural importance was swelled into greater, but without an artificial appearance. Its banks were neither formal, nor falsely adorned. Elizabeth was delighted. She had never seen a place for which nature had done more, or where natural beauty had been so little counteracted by an awkward taste. They were all of them warm in their admiration; and at that moment she felt, that to be mistress of Pemberley might be something!

. . . The housekeeper came; a respectable-looking, elderly woman, much less fine, and more civil, than she had any notion of finding her. They followed her into the dining-parlour. It was a large, well-proportioned room, handsomely fitted up. Elizabeth, after slightly surveying it, went to a window to enjoy its prospect. The hill, crowned with wood, from which they had descended, receiving increased abruptness from the distance, was a beautiful object. Every disposition of the ground was good; and she looked on the whole scene, the river, the trees scattered on its banks, and the winding of the valley, as far as she could trace it, with delight. As they passed into other rooms, these objects were taking different positions; but from every window there were beauties to be seen. The rooms were lofty and handsome, and their furniture suitable to the fortune of their proprietor; but Elizabeth saw, with admiration of his taste, that it was neither gaudy nor uselessly fine.

B

About half-way between West Egg and New York the motor road hastily joins the railroad and runs beside it for a quarter of a mile, so as to shrink away from a certain desolate area of land. This is a valley of ashes – a fantastic farm where ashes grow like wheat into ridges and hills and grotesque gardens; where ashes take the forms of houses and chimneys and rising smoke and, finally, with a transcendent effort, of ash-grey men, who move dimly and already crumbling through the powdery air. Occasionally a line of grey cars crawls along an invisible track, gives out a ghastly creak, and comes to rest, and immediately the ash-grey men swarm up with leaden spades and stir up an impenetrable cloud, which screens their obscure operations from your sight.

But above the grey land and the spasms of bleak dust which drift endlessly over it, you perceive, after a moment, the eyes of Doctor T. J. Eckleburg. The eyes of Doctor T. J. Eckleburg are blue and gigantic – their retinas are one yard high. They look out of no face, but, instead, from a pair of enormous yellow spectacles which pass over a non-existent nose. Evidently some wild wag of an oculist set them there to fatten his practice in the borough of Queens, and then sank down himself into eternal blindness, or forgot them and moved away. But his eyes, dimmed a little by many paintless days, under sun and rain, brood on over the solemn dumping ground.

C   *Court of Hill*

1 m. N of Nash

Fine sturdy brick house dated 1683. Seven bays, two storeys, hipped roof. Quoins of stone and stone trim of windows and doorway, probably altered. The windows presumably were of the cross-type originally. Handsome eaves-coving. Timber staircase with square open well and heavy balusters; still occasional Jacobean details. Diagonal board covering the tread-ends. Fine principal door-case on the first floor. Panelling and overmantel in the former entrance hall Jacobean or a little later and no doubt brought in. Partly restored. In one room a remarkable early c19 plaster ceiling, coffered and with much honeysuckle as well as naturalistic friezes of oak and vine. DOVECOTE, octagonal with pretty lead lantern. KITCHEN GARDEN. Entrance at the back of a Georgian pavilion with a front of Tuscan columns and pediment.

24

Miners

There was a whispering in my hearth,
    A sigh of the coal,
Grown wistful of a former earth
    It might recall.

I listened for a tale of leaves
    And smothered ferns;
Frond-forests; and the low, sly lives
    Before the fawns.

My fire might show steam-phantoms simmer
    From Time's old cauldron,
Before the birds made nests in summer,
    Or men had children.

But the coals were murmuring of their mine,
    And moans down there
Of boys that slept wry sleep, and men
    Writhing for air.

And I saw white bones in the cinder-shard.
    Bones without number;
For many hearts with coal are charred
    And few remember.

I thought of some who worked dark pits
    Of war, and died
Digging the rock where Death reputes
    Peace lies indeed.

Comforted years will sit soft-chaired
    In rooms of amber;
The years will stretch their hands, well-cheered
    By our lives' ember.

The centuries will burn rich loads
    With which we groaned,

Whose warmth shall lull their dreaming lids
   While songs are crooned.
But they will not dream of us poor lads
   Lost in the ground.

25

A   *The Funeral Rites of the Rose*

The rose was sick and smiling died;
And, being to be sanctified,
About the bed there sighing stood
The sweet and flowery sisterhood:
Some hung the head, while some did bring,
To wash her, water from the spring;
Some laid her forth, while others wept,
But all a solemn fast there kept:
The holy sisters, some among,
The sacred dirge and trental sung.
But ah! what sweets smelt everywhere,
As Heaven had spent all perfumes there.
At last, when prayers for the dead
And rites were all accomplished,
They, weeping, spread a lawny loom,
And closed her up as in a tomb.

B   *The Sick Rose*

O Rose, thou art sick!
The invisible worm
That flies in the night,
In the howling storm,

Has found out thy bed
Of crimson joy,
And his dark secret love
Does thy life destroy.

... The bell rang and then the classes began to file out of the rooms and along the corridors towards the refectory. He sat looking at the two prints of butter on his plate but could not eat the damp bread. The tablecloth was damp and limp. But he drank off the hot weak tea which the clumsy scullion, girt with a white apron, poured into his cup. He wondered whether the scullion's apron was damp too or whether all white things were cold and damp. Nasty Roche and Saurin drank cocoa that their people sent them in tins. They said they could not drink the tea; that it was hogwash. Their fathers were magistrates, the fellows said.

All the boys seemed to him very strange. They had all fathers and mothers and different clothes and voices. He longed to be at home and lay his head on his mother's lap, but he could not! and so he longed for the play and study and prayers to be over and to be in bed.

He drank another cup of hot tea and Fleming said:

— What's up? Have you a pain or what's up with you?

— I don't know, Stephen said.

— Sick in your breadbasket, Fleming said, because your face looks white. It will go away.

— O yes, Stephen said.

But he was not sick there. He thought that he was sick in his heart if you could be sick in that place. Fleming was very decent to ask him. He wanted to cry. He leaned his elbows on the table and shut and opened the flaps of his ears. Then he heard the noise of the refectory every time he opened the flaps of his ears. It made a roar like a train at night. And when he closed the flaps the roar was shut off like a train going into a tunnel. That night at Dalkey the train had roared like that and then, when it went into the tunnel, the roar stopped. He closed his eyes and the train went on, roaring and then stopping; roaring again, stopping. It was nice to hear it roar and stop and then roar out of the tunnel again and then stop.

Then the higher line fellows began to come down along the matting in the middle of the refectory.

[This follows a quarrel in which Eddie, Catherine's uncle and guardian, has betrayed jealousy of her boy friend, who is a cousin of Eddie's wife Beatrice. He is an illegal immigrant. Eddie has left the room.]

Beatrice. Listen, Catherine. *Catherine halts, turns to her sheepishly.* What are you going to do with yourself?

Catherine. I don't know.

Beatrice. Don't tell me you don't know; you're not a baby any more, what are you going to do with yourself?

Catherine. He won't listen to me.

Beatrice. I don't understand this. He's not your father, Catherine, I don't understand what's going on here.

Catherine as one who is herself trying to rationalise a buried impulse. What am I going to do, just kick him in the face with it?

Beatrice. Look, honey, you wanna get married, or don't you wanna get married? What are you worried about, Katie?

Catherine quietly, trembling. I don't know B. It just seems wrong if he's against it so much.

Beatrice never losing her aroused alarm. Sit down, honey, I want to tell you something. Here, sit down. Was there ever any fella he liked for you? There wasn't, was there?

Catherine. But he says Rodolpho's just after his papers.

Beatrice. Look, he'll say anything. What does he care what he says? If it was a prince came here for you it would be no different. You know that, don't you?

Catherine. Yeah, I guess.

Beatrice. So what does that mean?

Catherine slowly turns her head to Beatrice. What?

Beatrice. It means you gotta be your own self more. You still think you're a little girl, honey. But nobody else can make up your mind for you any more, you understand? You gotta give him to understand that he can't give you orders no more.

Catherine. Yeah, but how am I going to do that? He thinks I'm a baby.

Beatrice. Because *you* think you're a baby. . . .

28

In My Craft or Sullen Art

In my craft or sullen art
Exercised in the still night
When only the moon rages
And the lovers lie abed
With all their griefs in their arms,
I labour by singing light
Not for ambition or bread
Or the strut and trade of charms
On the ivory stages
But for the common wages
Of their most secret heart.

Not for the proud man apart
From the raging moon I write
On these spindrift pages
Nor for the towering dead
With their nightingales and psalms
But for the lovers, their arms
Round the griefs of the ages,
Who pay no praise or wages
Nor heed my craft or art.

29

A
Troublesome Fame

To be born famous, as your father's son,
   Is a fate troublesome enough, unless
Like Philip's Alexander of Macedon
   You can out-do him by superb excess
Of greed and profligacy and wantonness.

To become famous as a wonder-child
   Brings no less trouble, with whatever art

You toyed precociously, for Fame had smiled
    Malevolence at your birth . . . Only Mozart
Played on, still smiling from his placid heart.

To become famous while a raw young man
    And lead Fame by the nose, to a bitter end,
As Caesar's nephew did, Octavian
    Styling himself Augustus, is to pretend
Peace in the torments that such laurels lend.

To become famous in your middle years
    For merit not unblessed by accident –
Encountering cat-calls, missiles, jeers and sneers
    From half your uncontrollable parliament –
Is no bad fate, to a good sportsman sent. . . .

But Fame attendant on extreme old age
    Falls best. What envious youth cares to compete
With a lean sage hauled painfully upstage,
    Bowing, gasping, shuffling his frozen feet –
A ribboned hearse parked plainly down the street?

B   *To ——*

    You might have won the Poet's name
    If such be worth the winning now,
    And gain'd a laurel for your brow
    Of sounder leaf than I can claim;

    But you have made the wiser choice,
    A life that moves to gracious ends
    Thro' troops of unrecording friends,
    A deedful life, a silent voice:

    And you have miss'd the irreverent doom
    Of those that wear the Poet's crown:
    Hereafter, neither knave nor clown
    Shall hold their orgies at your tomb.

    For now the Poet cannot die,
    Nor leave his music as of old,

But round him ere he scarce be cold
Begins the scandal and the cry:

'Proclaim the faults he would not show,
Break lock and seal: betray the trust:
Keep nothing sacred: 'tis but just
The many-headed beast should know.'

Ah shameless! for he did but sing
A song that pleased us from its worth;
No public life was his on earth,
No blazon'd statesman he, nor king.

He gave the people of his best:
His worst he kept, his best he gave.
My Shakespeare's curse on clown and knave
Who will not let his ashes rest!

Who make it seem more sweet to be
The little life of bank and brier,
The bird that pipes his lone desire
And dies unheard within his tree,

Than he that warbles long and loud
And drops at Glory's temple-gates,
For whom the carrion vulture waits
To tear his heart before the crowd!

C   *Growing Old*

What is it to grow old?
Is it to lose the glory of the form,
The lustre of the eye?
Is it for beauty to forego her wreath?
– Yes, not this alone.

Is it to feel our strength –
Not our bloom only, but our strength – decay?
Is it to feel each limb
Grow stiffer, every function less exact,
Each nerve more loosely strung?

Yes, this, and more; but not
Ah, 'tis not what in youth we dream'd 'twould be!
'Tis not to have our life
Mellow'd and soften'd as with sunset-glow
A golden day's decline.

'Tis not to see the world
As from a height, with rapt prophetic eyes,
And heart profoundly stirr'd;
And weep, and feel the fulness of the past,
The years that are no more.

It is to spend long days
And not once feel that we were ever young;
It is to add, immured
In the hot prison of the present, month
To month with weary pain.

It is to suffer this,
And feel but half, and feebly, what we feel.
Deep in our hidden heart
Festers the dull remembrance of a change,
But no emotion – none.

It is – last stage of all –
When we are frozen up within, and quite
The phantom of ourselves,
To hear the world applaud the hollow ghost
Which blamed the living man.

30

The Death of Paul Dombey

[The following passage from *Dombey and Son* was used by Dickens in his immensely popular public readings of his own works. Walter Gay was a young clerk in Dombey's office. Although a cheerful and industrious employee, he was resented by Paul Dombey's father, partly because of the contrast between him and the sickly Paul. Mr.

Dombey also disapproved of Walter's friendship with his daughter Florence ('Floy') whom Walter had helped when she was a little child. The parts in italics were omitted from the reading version.]

'Thank you, Floy!' . . .

Then he woke – woke mind and body – and sat upright in bed. He saw them now about him. There was no grey mist before them, as there had been sometimes in the night. He knew them every one, and called them by their names.

'And who is this? Is this my old nurse?' said the child, regarding with a radiant smile, a figure coming in.

Yes, yes. No other stranger would have shed those tears at sight of him, and called him her dear boy, her pretty boy, her own poor blighted child. No other woman would have stooped down by his bed, and taken up his wasted hand, and put it to her lips and breast, as one who had some right to fondle it. No other woman would have so forgotten everybody there but him and Floy, and been so full of tenderness and pity.

'Floy! this is a kind good face!' said Paul. 'I am glad to see it again. Don't go away, old nurse! Stay here.'

His senses were all quickened, and he heard a name he knew.

'Who was that, who said "Walter"?' he asked, looking round 'Some one said "Walter". Is he here? I should like to see him very much.'

Nobody replied directly; but his father soon said to Susan, 'Call him back, then: let him come up!' After a short pause of expectation, during which he looked with smiling interest and wonder on his nurse, and saw that she had not forgotten Floy, Walter was brought into the room. His open face and manner, and his cheerful eyes, had always made him a favourite with Paul; and when Paul saw him, he stretched out his hand, and said 'Good-bye!'

'Good-bye, my child!' cried Mrs. Pipchin, hurrying to his bed's head. 'Not good-bye?'

For an instant, Paul looked at her with the wistful face with which he had so often gazed upon her in his corner by the fire. 'Ah, yes,' he said placidly, 'good-bye!' '*Walter dear, good-bye!*' – *turning his head to where he stood, and putting out his hand again.* 'Where is papa?'

He felt his father's breath upon his cheek, before the words had parted from his lips.

'*Remember Walter, dear papa,*' *he whispered, looking in his face.* '*Remember Walter. I was fond of Walter!*' The feeble hand waved in the air, as if it cried 'good-bye' *to Walter once again.*

'Now lay me down,' he said, 'and Floy, come close to me, and let me see you!'

Sister and brother wound their arms around each other, and the golden light came streaming in, and fell upon them, locked together.

'How fast the river runs, between its green banks and the rushes, Floy! But it's very near the sea. I hear the waves! They always said so!'

Presently he told her that the motion of the boat upon the stream was lulling him to rest. How green the banks were now, how bright the flowers growing on them, and how tall the rushes! Now the boat was out at sea, but gliding smoothly on. And now there was a shore before him. Who stood on the bank?

He put his hands together, as he had been used to do at his prayers. He did not remove his arms to do it; but they saw him fold them so, behind her neck.

'Mamma is like you, Floy. I know her by the face! But tell them that the print upon the stairs at school is not divine enough. The light about the head is shining on me as I go!'

The golden ripple on the wall came back again, and nothing else stirred in the room. The old, old fashion! The fashion that came in with our first garments, and will last unchanged until our race has run its course, and the wide firmament is rolled up like a scroll. The old, old fashion – Death!

O thank GOD, all who see it, for that older fashion yet, of Immortality! And look upon us, angels of young children, with regards not quite estranged, when the swift river bears us to the ocean!

31

A   *Upon Westminster Bridge*

> Earth has not anything to show more fair:
> Dull would he be of soul who could pass by
> A sight so touching in its majesty:

This City now doth, like a garment, wear
The beauty of the morning; silent, bare,
Ships, towers, domes, theatres, and temples lie
Open unto the fields, and to the sky;
All bright and glittering in the smokeless air.
Never did sun more beautifully steep
In his first splendour, valley, rock, or hill;
Ne'er saw I, never felt, a calm so deep!
The river glideth at his own sweet will;
Dear God! the very houses seem asleep;
And all that mighty heart is lying still!

B

Poet On The Brink

Calm autumn night, seen from a high window.
Above the roofs, the trees, an urban sky
Breathed-on and fogged with light; a notched horizon
Printed black; spread behind leaves, transparent
Fans of lamp-gold; a clock-tower, white as bone,
Rapt in a floodlit trance; and over all
A gritty hush, a solvent monotone.

The clock strikes peace – and any moment now
West 3 will beg a sonnet. Just remember
What's going on down there, and let it beg.
Most certainly the very houses seem,
And all that mighty heart is lying – still.
Even amid such trees the fluting owl
Glides velvet through the darkness to his kill.

32

A

The Least of These

'Lord, in Thy Courts
Are seats so green bestow'd,
As there resorts
Along the dusty road

A cavalcade, – King, Bishop, Knight, and Judge:
And though I toil behind and meanly trudge,
Let me, too, lie upon that pleasant sward,
 For I am weary, Lord.

 'Christ, at thy board
 Are wines and dishes drest
 That do afford
 Contentment to the best.
And though with poverty my bed hath been
These many years and my refreshment lean,
With plenty now at last my soul acquaint,
 Dear Master, for I faint!'

 But through the grille,
 'Where is thy Robe?' said He,
 'Wouldst eat thy fill,
 Yet shirk civility?'
'My Robe, alas! There was a little child
That shivered by the road' – Swiftly God smiled;
'I was that Child,' said He, and raised the pin;
 Dear friend, enter thou in!'

B   *Love*

Love bade me welcome; yet my soul drew back,
 Guilty of dust and sin.
But quick-eyed Love, observing me grow slack
 From my first entrance in,
Drew nearer to me, sweetly questioning
 If I lack'd anything.

'A guest,' I answer'd, 'worthy to be here':
 Love said, 'You shall be he.'
'I, the unkind, ungrateful? Ah, my dear,
 I cannot look on Thee.'
Love took my hand and smiling did reply,
 'Who made the eyes but I?'

'Truth, Lord; but I have marr'd them; let my shame
    Go where it doth deserve.'
'And know you not,' says Love. 'Who bore the blame?'
    'My dear, then I will serve.'
'You must sit down,' says Love, 'and taste my meat.'
    So I did sit and eat.

33

[Willie, a butcher, is talking to Rose, his son's girl-friend.]

Rose.   You said you could talk to me.

Willie.   Yes –

Rose.   Well then. Interest me.

Willie.   My idea of what's romantic – it might not be the same as yours.

Rose.   I find lots of things romantic.

Willie.   Romance is – often in small things –

Rose.   Yes. Go on.

Willie.   Insignificant things. For instance, the way you held your hands away from Clive, your nails, you'd been doing them –

Rose.   They were barely dry – (she holds her hands, as though the nails are newly varnished).

Willie.   It was the way you held them out –

Rose.   Well go on Willie, that's not much.

Willie.   No. I know. But holding your hands like that, put you in a certain way –

Rose.   Oh?

Willie.   Different from if you'd come at him clutching him. You never touched him with your hands that time. He wasn't aware, though. Another thing, later you came in, you said about watching the stars, and then opened up your coat and sat down.

Rose.   So?

Willie.   I found that romantic.

Rose.   What little things!

Willie.   I told you –

Rose.   But nice – I do like them.

Willie. If you add up all the little things –

Rose. Most people ignore 'em all –

Willie. Yes –

Rose. But you don't. You add them up.

Willie. Yes –

Rose. Well go on Willie. Some more.

Willie. Some things, you can't hardly explain to somebody else.

Rose. Not even me?

Willie. It's hard. You don't know what they mean yourself. For instance, you said 'I'm me, I'm Rosemary Duke' –

Rose. That's me, yes. That's right.

Willie. Yes. But it was more than that, just your name. It – I – it made me feel sorry for you –

Rose. I don't understand that.

Willie. No. I don't. But just only repeating it, I get this same feeling of pity for you –

Rose. You've nothing to feel sorry for me.

34

April 25. In consequence of Brickwell telling me his wife was working wonders with the new Pinkford's enamel paint, I determined to try it. I bought two tins of red on my way home. I hastened through tea, went into the garden and painted some flower-pots. I called out Carrie, who said: 'You've always got some new-fangled craze'; but she was obliged to admit that the flower-pots looked remarkably well. Went upstairs into the servant's bedroom and painted her washstand, towel-horse, and chest of drawers. To my mind it was an extraordinary improvement, but as an example of the ignorance of the lower classes in the matter of taste, our servant, Sarah, on seeing them, evinced no sign of pleasure, but merely said 'she thought they looked very well as they was before'.

April 26. Got some more red enamel paint (red, to my mind, being the best colour), and painted the coal-scuttle, and the backs of our *Shakespeare*, the binding of which had almost worn out.

April 27. Painted the bath red, and was delighted with the result. Sorry to say Carrie was not, in fact we had a few words about it.

She said I ought to have consulted her, and she had never heard of such a thing as a bath being painted red. I replied: 'It's merely a matter of taste.' . . .

April 29, Sunday. Woke up with a fearful headache and strong symptoms of a cold. Carrie, with a perversity which is just like her, said it was 'painter's colic', and was the result of my having spent the last few days with my nose over a paint-pot. I told her firmly that I knew a great deal better what was the matter with me than she did. I had got a chill and decided to have a bath as hot as I could bear it. Bath ready – could scarcely bear it so hot. I persevered, and got in; very hot, but very acceptable. I lay still for some time. On moving my hand above the surface of the water, I experienced the greatest fright I ever received in the whole course of my life; for imagine my horror on discovering my hand, as I thought, full of blood. My first thought was that I had ruptured an artery, and was bleeding to death, and should be discovered, later on, looking like a second Marat, as I remember seeing him in Madame Tussaud's. My second thought was to ring the bell, but remembered there was no bell to ring. My third was, that there was nothing but the enamel paint, which had dissolved with boiling water. I stepped out of the bath, perfectly red all over, resembling the Red Indians I have seen depicted at an East-End theatre. I determined not to say a word to Carrie, but to tell Farmerson to come on Monday and paint the bath white.

35

The boy who resided at Agathox Lodge, 27, Buckingham Park Road, Surbiton, had often been puzzled by the old sign-post that stood almost opposite. . . . For there were two strange things about this sign-post: firstly, it pointed up a blank alley, and, secondly, it had painted on it, in faded characters, the words, 'To Heaven.' . . .

It struck him . . . that he might do worse than ask Mr. Bons about the sign-post. . . . Mr. Bons was serious as well as kind. He had a beautiful house and lent one books, he was a church-warden, and a candidate for the County Council; he had donated to the Free Library enormously, he presided over the Literary Society, and had

Members of Parliament to stop with him – in short, he was probably the wisest person alive.

Yet even Mr. Bons could only say that the sign-post was a joke – the joke of a person named Shelley.

'Of course!' cried the mother; 'I told you so, dear. That was the name.'

'Had you never heard of Shelley?' asked Mr. Bons.

'No,' said the boy, and hung his head.

'But is there no Shelley in the house?'

'Why, yes!' exclaimed the lady, in much agitation. 'Dear Mr. Bons, we aren't such Philistines as that. Two at the least. One a wedding present, and the other, smaller print, in one of the spare rooms.'

'I believe we have seven Shelleys,' said Mr. Bons, with a slow smile. Then he brushed the cake crumbs off his stomach, and, together with his daughter, rose to go.

36

A   *Time*

Unfathomable Sea! whose waves are years,
Ocean of Time, whose waters of deep woe
Are brackish with the salt of human tears!
Thou shoreless flood, which in thy ebb and flow
Claspest the limits of mortality,
And sick of prey, yet howling on for more,
Vomitest thy wrecks on its inhospitable shore;
Treacherous in calm, and terrible in storm,
Who shall put forth on thee,
Unfathomable Sea?

B   *Dover Beach*

The sea is calm to-night.
The tide is full, the moon lies fair
Upon the straits; – on the French coast the light

Gleams and is gone; the cliffs of England stand,
Glimmering and vast, out in the tranquil bay.
Come to the window, sweet is the night-air!
Only, from the long line of spray
Where the sea meets the moon-blanch'd land,
Listen! you hear the grating roar
Of pebbles which the waves draw back, and fling,
At their return, up the high strand,
Begin, and cease, and then again begin,
With tremulous cadence slow, and bring
The eternal note of sadness in.

Sophocles long ago
Heard it on the Aegean, and it brought
Into his mind the turbid ebb and flow
Of human misery; we
Find also in the sound a thought,
Hearing it by this distant northern sea.

The Sea of Faith
Was once, too, at the full, and round earth's shore
Lay like the folds of a bright girdle furl'd.
But now I only hear
Its melancholy, long, withdrawing roar,
Retreating, to the breath
Of the night-wind, down the vast edges drear
And naked shingles of the world.
Ah, love, let us be true
To one another! for the world, which seems
To lie before us like a land of dreams,
So various, so beautiful, so new,
Hath really neither joy, nor love, nor light,
Nor certitude, nor peace, nor help for pain;
And we are here as on a darkling plain
Swept with confused alarms of struggle and flight,
Where ignorant armies clash by night.

37

A

My God! Can it be possible I have
To die so suddenly? So young to go
Under the obscure, cold, rotting, wormy ground!
To be nailed down into a narrow place;
To see no more sweet sunshine; hear no more
Blithe voice of living thing; muse not again
Upon familiar thoughts, sad, yet thus lost –
How fearful! to be nothing! Or to be . . .
What? Oh, where am I? Let me not go mad!
Sweet Heaven, forgive weak thoughts! If there should be
No God, no Heaven, no Earth in the void world;
The wide, gray, lampless, deep, unpeopled world!

B

Ay, but to die, and go we know not where,
To lie in cold obstruction and to rot;
This sensible warm motion to become
A kneaded clod; and the delighted spirit
To bathe in fiery floods, or to reside
In thrilling region of thick-ribbed ice;
To be imprison'd in the viewless winds,
And blown with restless violence round about
The pendent world; or to be worse than worst
Of those that lawless and incertain thoughts
Imagine howling: 'tis too horrible!
The weariest and most loathed earthly life
That age, ache, penury and imprisonment
Can lay on nature is a paradise
To what we fear of death.

[A black South African schoolteacher talks with the woman he loves, a white librarian.]

Man. I'll tell you something else. Coming here once . . . in the 'old' days . . . I passed a man and a woman and their child . . . little boy . . . going back to the location. They got names, but it doesn't matter. You don't know them. They had stopped half-way up the hill to rest. It's hard walking up there with the sun on your back. All three of them . . . hot and unwashed. They smell. Because I was coming to you, you know what I saw? Rags. I don't mean their clothes. The people inside looked like rags. The man drinks too much, he's a useless rag. The woman's an old rag. Their child is going to be somebody's good rag, until. . . . What do you do with yours? I was looking at my feet when I walked past them. Frieda! . . . (shaking his head) . . . when I realized that . . . when I realized what I . . . I wanted to call them and bring them with me to the library. I wanted to knock on that back door and stand there with them when you opened it. I wanted you to see me with them! What would you have done? Asked them in? Called them Miester and Meisies? Would you have given them tea in your cups? How long before you would have started waiting for them to go? You understand now. The reason I don't want your water is just because Bontrug is thirsty.

Woman. And that is not pride.

Man. No. Exactly the opposite. Shame.

Woman. I don't understand . . . anything.

Man. Then you can't. Don't even try. (*He turns away from her back to his clothes and puts on his vest.*)

Woman. It really would be better if you could wait until it's darker. (*He stops. Pause.*) Old Mrs. Buys is still staring and being strange. She changed her books again today. I might be wrong but . . . She's taken out more books this month than she did the whole of last year.

Man. And you think I'm proud.

Woman. You should be . . . of some things.

39

A

No longer mourn for me when I am dead
Than you shall hear the surly sullen bell
Give warning to the world that I am fled
From this vile world, with vilest worms to dwell.
Nay, if you read this line, remember not
The hand that writ it; for I love you so,
That I in your sweet thoughts would be forgot,
If thinking on me then should make you woe.
O, if, I say, you look upon this verse,
When I perhaps compounded am with clay,
Do not so much as my poor name rehearse,
But let your love even with my life decay;
Lest the wise world should look into your moan,
And mock you with me after I am gone.

B

Remember me when I am gone away,
Gone far away into the silent land;
When you can no more hold me by the hand,
Nor I half turn to go, yet turning stay.
Remember me when no more day by day
You tell me of our future that you plann'd:
Only remember me; you understand
It will be late to counsel then or pray.
Yet if you should forget me for a while
And afterwards remember, do not grieve:
For if the darkness and corruption leave
A vestige of the thoughts that once I had,
Better by far you should forget and smile
Than that you should remember and be sad.

40

A

As in all David Jones's work the sharpness of focus with which the
details are seen varies from inch to inch. I am reminded of the

hours I used to spend fishing off the coast of Skye, when, on calm days, one could look down many fathoms to gently undulating streamers of weed, sea-urchins, sea-anemones and puffs of sand, where the furtive flounder burrowed its way out of sight. Then a breeze would ruffle the surface and this garden of delights would be disturbed, but through a window of calm water one could still catch sight of certain man-defined objects, an old anchor or a discarded rowlock. So, in David Jones's drawing, the welter of clouds, seagulls and stars that surrounds Tristan's ship seems to be ruffled by the wind, but on the ship itself the mechanism of sail is made clear, with anchors, blocks and a contrivance known as a knight-head, drawn as sharply as Iseult's foot.

B

The presence that thus rose so strangely beside the waters is expressive of what in the ways of a thousand years men had come to desire. Hers is the head upon which all 'the ends of the world are come', and the eyelids are a little weary. It is a beauty wrought out from within upon the flesh, the deposit, little cell by little cell, of strange thoughts and fantastic reveries and exquisite passions. Set it for a moment beside one of those white Greek goddesses or beautiful women of antiquity, and how could they be troubled by this beauty, into which the soul with all its maladies has passed? All the thoughts and experience of the world have etched and moulded there, in that which they have of power to refine and make expressive the outward form, the animalism of Greece, the lust of Rome, the reverie of the middle age with its spiritual ambition and imaginative loves, the return of the Pagan world, the sins of the Borgias. She is older than the rocks among which she sits; like the vampire, she has been dead many times, and learned the secrets of the grave; and has been a diver in deep seas, and keeps their fallen day about her; trafficked for strange webs with Eastern merchants: and, as Leda, was the mother of Helen of Troy, and, as Saint Anne, the mother of Mary; and all this has been to her but as the sound of lyres and flutes, and lives only in the delicacy with which it has moulded the changing lineaments and tinged the eyelids and the hands.

41

A   *Highway: Michigan*

Here from the field's edge we survey
The progress of the jaded. Mile
On mile of traffic from the town
Rides by, for at the end of the day
The time of workers is their own.

They jockey for position on
The strip reserved for passing only.
The drivers from production lines
Hold to advantage dearly won.
They toy with death and traffic fines.

Acceleration is their need:
A mania keeps them on the move
Until the toughest nerves are frayed.
They are the prisoners of speed
Who flee in what their hands have made.

The pavement smokes when two cars meet
And steel rips through conflicting steel.
We shiver at the siren's blast.
One driver, pinned beneath the seat,
Escapes from the machine at last.

B   *At Any Rate*

'He's dead,' they shouted as he left his motorbike
And catapulted twenty foot through air
And dented earth. They wanted him to be dead
Out of a sort of innocent malignance
And being born dramatists the lot of them.
And dead he was in the end. The blood gushed
From his ears. 'He's dead,' they told the doctor,
Though he wasn't, as the doctor saw at once,

By any means dead. 'Officer,' they said, 'he's dead.
He ought to be, at any rate if he's human.'
And in the end they were right, dead right.
An hour later, by the tangled bike
(Considered by the crowd by no means done for)
They were still standing, very much alive –
As they ought to be, at any rate if they're human.

42

Praise

I praise you because
you are artist and scientist
in one. When I am somewhat
fearful of your power,
your ability to work miracles
with a set-square, I hear
you murmuring to yourself
in a notation Beethoven
dreamed of but never achieved.
You run off your scales of
rain water and sea water, play
the chords of the morning
and evening light, sculpture
with shadow, join together leaf
by leaf, when spring
comes, the stanzas of
an immense poem. You speak
all languages and none,
answering our most complex
prayers with the simplicity
of a flower, confronting
us, when we would domesticate you
to our uses, with the rioting
viruses under our lens.

43

[In this extract from a modern play derived from Shakespeare's *Hamlet*, Rosencrantz and Guildenstern are questioning the player, with a view to determining their own significance in relation to Hamlet's predicament.]

Guil. Where are you going?

Player. I can come and go as I please.

Guil. You're evidently a man who knows his way around.

Player. I've been here before.

Guil. We're still finding our feet.

Player. I should concentrate on not losing your heads.

Guil. Do you speak from knowledge?

Player. Precedent.

Guil. You've been here before.

Player. And I know which way the wind is blowing.

Guil. Operating on two levels, are we? How clever! I expect it comes naturally to you, being in the business so to speak. (*The Player's grave face does not change. He makes to move off again. Guil. for the second time cuts him off.*) The truth is, we value your company, for want of any other. We have been left so much to our own devices – after a while one welcomes the uncertainty of being left to other people's.

Player. Uncertainty is the normal state. You're nobody special. (*He makes to leave again. Guil. loses his cool.*)

Guil. But for God's sake what are we supposed to *do*?!

Player. Relax. Respond. That's what people do. You can't go through life questioning your situation at every turn.

Guil. But we don't know what's going on, or what to do with ourselves. We don't know how to *act*.

Player. Act natural. You know why you're here at least.

Guil. We only know what we're told, and that's little enough. And for all we know it isn't even true.

Player. For all anyone knows, nothing is. Everything has to be taken on trust; truth is only that which is taken to be true. It's the currency of living. There may be nothing behind it, but it doesn't make any difference so long as it is honoured. One acts on assumptions. What do you assume?

Ros. Hamlet is not himself, outside or in. We have to glean what afflicts him.

Guil. He doesn't give much away.

Player. Who does, nowadays?

Guil. He's – melancholy.

Player. Melancholy?

Ros. Mad.

Player. How is he mad?

Ros. Ah. (*To Guil.*) How is he mad?

Guil. More morose than mad, perhaps.

Player. Melancholy.

Guil. Moody.

Ros. He has moods.

Player. Of moroseness?

Guil. Madness. And yet.

Ros. Quite.

Guil. For instance.

Ros. He talks to himself, which might be madness.

Guil. If he didn't talk sense, which he does.

Ros. Which suggests the opposite.

44

Strange Meeting

It seemed that out of battle I escaped
Down some profound dull tunnel, long since scooped
Through granites which titanic wars had groined.
Yet also there encumbered sleepers groaned,
Too fast in thought or death to be bestirred.
Then, as I probed them, one sprang up, and stared
With piteous recognition in fixed eyes,
Lifting distressful hands as if to bless.
And by his smile, I knew that sullen hall,
By his dead smile I knew we stood in Hell.

With a thousand pains that vision's face was grained;
Yet no blood reached there from the upper ground,
And no guns thumped, or down the flues made moan.
'Strange friend,' I said, 'here is no cause to mourn.'
'None,' said that other, 'save the undone years,
The hopelessness. Whatever hope is yours,
Was my life also; I went hunting wild
After the wildest beauty in the world,
Which lies not calm in eyes, or braided hair,
But mocks the steady running of the hour,
And if it grieves, grieves richlier than here.
For of my glee might many men have laughed,
And of my weeping something had been left,
Which must die now. I mean the truth untold,
The pity of war, the pity war distilled.
Now men will go content with what we spoiled,
Or, discontent, boil bloody, and be spilled.
They will be swift with swiftness of the tigress.
None will break ranks, though nations trek from progress.
Courage was mine, and I had mystery,
Wisdom was mine, and I had mastery:
To miss the march of this retreating world
Into vain citadels that are not walled.
Then, when much blood had clogged their chariot-wheels,
I would go up and wash them from sweet wells,
Even with truths that lie too deep for taint.
I would have poured my spirit without stint
But not through wounds; not on the cess of war.
Foreheads of men have bled where no wounds were.
I am the enemy you killed, my friend.
I knew you in this dark: for so you frowned
Yesterday through me as you jabbed and killed.
I parried; but my hands were loath and cold.
Let us sleep now. . . .'

45

A

We cast the net of our own language over the multiplicity of living forms. Loosely woven, it will draw in experience in gross, indiscriminate lumps; the landscape of being is made incoherent and monotonous by illiterate speech. Close knit, the language-net makes available to us the largest possible range – possible to our physiological and historical condition – of differentiated, mastered, potentially related elements.

A large vocabulary signifies a literal wealth and concreteness of felt life. A developed syntax engenders those perceptions of inter-relation, those creative re-groupings of thought and action called metaphor. Without metaphor a society remains static, repetitive, as is a child's song. Our world, the way we move among its total possibilities, springs from grammar, from the pattern by which we relate identity, verb and object. Each grammar differs in some degree from any other. . . . No two languages mesh perfectly, no two languages – and there may be some three thousand spoken by men – set the world in the same order.

Even the simplest words, indeed they especially, carry a charge of specific energy, of historical association, social usage and syntactic tradition. They rise to the surface of speech from great depths of national or regional sensibility, barnacled with undeclared remembrance. *Pain* is not wholly rendered by *bread*. It has to a French ear resonances of want, of radical demand, which the English word does not; the two words differ in historical texture as does a French from an English loaf.

B   *To His Worthy Friend Doctor Witty Upon His*
      Translation Of The 'Popular Errors'

> Sit further, and make room for thine own fame,
> Where just desert enrolls thy honoured name –
> The good interpreter. Some in this task
> Take off the cypress veil, but leave a mask,
> Changing the Latin, but do more obscure
> That sense in English which was bright and pure.

So of translators they are authors grown,
For ill translators make the book their own.
Others do strive with words and forced phrase
To add such lustre, and so many rays,
That, but to make the vessel shining, they
Much of the precious metal rub away.
He is translation's thief that addeth more,
As much as he that taketh from the store
Of the first author. Here he maketh blots
That mends; and added beauties are but spots.
    Celia whose English doth more richly flow
Than Tagus, purer than dissolved snow,
And sweet as are her lips that speak it, she
Now learns the tongues of France and Italy;
But she is Celia still: no other grace
But her own smiles commend that lovely face;
Her native beauty's not Italianated,
Nor her chaste mind into the French translated:
Her thoughts are English, though her sparkling wit
With other language doth them fitly fit.
    Translators learn of her.

46

'You must be feeling peckish,' the expectant Mr. Bonner remarked.

'Please?' asked Voss, perhaps to avoid making a decision.

'I dare say' – the merchant gave it extra weight – 'you could put away your share of dinner.'

'I am not prepared,' replied the German, who was again unhappy.

'Who ever had to prepare for a plate of prime beef and pudding!' said the merchant, already surging forth. 'Mrs. Bonner,' he called, 'our friend will stay for dinner.'

'So I anticipated,' said Mrs. Bonner, 'and Rose has laid a place.'

The men had come out to her and, in fact, to all the company, who were now assembled in the cool hall, shifting their feet upon the yellow stone. Cool stone drank the laughter of the young people, and their conversation . . . And there were the Palethorpes . . . Mr. P., as Mrs. Bonner would refer to him, was her husband's right hand, and indispensable as such, if also conveniently a Sunday joke. Mr. P. was bald, with a moustache that somewhat resembled a pair of dead birds. And there was his wife – she had been a governess – a most discreet person, whether in her choice of shawls, or behaviour, in the houses of the rich. The P.'s were waiting there, self-effacing, yet both at home, superior in the long practice of discretion.

'Thank you, I will not stay,' Voss said, now in anger.

A rude man, saw Mrs. Bonner.

A foreigner, saw the P.'s. . .

'You will not stay?' blustered the host, as if already potato-in-mouth.

'If that is the intention of Mr. Voss,' said Mrs. Bonner, 'then we shall sustain a loss.'

'You have made a bad poem!' laughed Belle, kissing at her mother's neck.

The young girl was inclined to ignore visitors when any of her family was present.

'The more beef for Mr. P.!' cried Lieutenant Radclyffe, who was chafing even in his humour.

'Why, pray, for Mr. P.?!' exclaimed the gentleman's wife in discreet protest, but giggled to please her patrons. 'Is he a lion, then?'

Everybody laughed. Even Mr. P. showed his teeth beneath his dead birds. He was a man of all purposes.

Consequently Voss was almost forgotten.

'I am already bidden,' he said.

Although it was really unnecessary to assure those who were so little anxious for assurance.

Expectation was goaded by smells that drifted past the cedar doors, with the consequence that the yellow flags were becoming intolerable to most feet.

'Then, if Mr. Voss is already engaged,' said Mrs. Bonner, to release someone who was unacquainted with the convolutions of polite behaviour.

'Too bad, old Voss!' said the brisk Lieutenant, who would

cheerfully have abandoned this unnecessary acquaintance, to rush in himself, slash with a sword at the sirloin, and watch the red juices run . . .

Sooner or later he was leaving, through the laughter and conversation of ladies, who had entered the dining-room, and were recalling the sermon and bonnets, as they seated themselves upon the chairs to which gentlemen blindly assisted them.

47

A Coal Fire in Winter

Something old and tyrannical burning there.
(Not like a wood fire which is only
The end of a summer, or a life)
But something of darkness: heat
From the time before there was fire.
And I have come here
To warm that blackness into forms of light,
To set free a captive prince
From the sunken kingdom of the father coal.

A warming company of the cold-blooded —
These carbon serpents of bituminous gardens,
These inflammable tunnels of dead song from the black pit,
This sparkling end of the great beasts, these blazing
Stone flowers diamond fire incandescent fruit.
And out of all that death, now,
At midnight, my love and I are riding
Down the old high roads of inexhaustible light.

48

A

What is our life? A play of passion,
Our mirth the music of division.
Our mothers' wombs the tiring-houses be,
Where we are dressed for this short comedy.

Heaven the judicious sharp spectator is,
That sits and marks still who doth act amiss.
Our graves that hide us from the searching sun
Are like drawn curtains when the play is done.
Thus march we, playing, to our latest rest,
Only we die in earnest, that's no jest.

B

Tell me, tell me, smiling child,
What the past is like to thee?
'An Autumn evening soft and mild
With a wind that sighs mournfully.'

Tell me, what is the present hour?
'A green and flowery spray
Where a young bird sits gathering its power
To mount and fly away.'

And what is the future, happy one?
'A sea beneath a cloudless sun;
A mighty, glorious, dazzling sea
Stretching into infinity.'

49

A

. . . The car ran on along the uplands, seeing the rolling county
spread out. The county! It had once been a proud and lordly county.
In front, looming again and hanging on the brow of the sky-line,
was the huge and splendid bulk of Chadwick Hall, more window
than wall, one of the most famous Elizabethan houses. Noble it
stood alone above a great park, but out of date, passed over. It was
still kept up, but as a show place. 'Look how our ancestors lorded
it!'

That was the past. The present lay below. God alone knows
where the future lies. The car was already turning, between little
old blackened miners' cottages, to descend to Uthwaite. And
Uthwaite, on a damp day, was sending up a whole array of smoke

plumes and steam to whatever gods there be. Uthwaite down in the valley, with all the steel threads of the railways to Sheffield drawn through it, and the coal-mines and the steel-works sending up smoke and glare from long tubes, and the pathetic little corkscrew spire of the church, that is going to tumble down, still pricking the fumes, always affected Connie strangely. It was an old market-town, centre of the dales. One of the chief inns was the Chatterley Arms. There, in Uthwaite, Wragby was known as Wragby, as if it were a whole place, not just a house, as it was to outsiders: Wragby Hall, near Tevershall: Wragby, a 'seat'.

The miners' cottages, blackened, stood flush on the pavement, with that intimacy and smallness of colliers' dwellings over a hundred years old. They lined all the way. The road had become a street, and as you sank, you forgot instantly the open, rolling country where the castles and big houses still dominated, but like ghosts. Now you were just above the tangle of naked railway-lines, and foundries and other 'works' rose about you, so big you were only aware of walls. And iron clanked with a huge reverberating clank, and huge lorries shook the earth, and whistles screamed.

Yet again, once you had got right down and into the twisted and crooked heart of the town, behind the church, you were in the world of two centuries ago, in the crooked streets where the Chatterley Arms stood, and the old pharmacy, streets which used to lead out to the wild open world of the castles and stately couchant houses.

But at the corner a policeman held up his hand as three lorries loaded with iron rolled past, shaking the poor old church. And not till the lorries were past could he salute her ladyship.

B

. . . As I sat there my mind went back suddenly, ten, no eleven years, to Stellenbosch. I could see the very room where we were sitting, five or six of us students, Moffie de Bruyn's room, with the old Vierkleur on the wall and the picture of President Kruger. We were talking of South Africa, as we always talked when it was not football or psychology or religion. We were talking of colour and race, and whether such feelings were born in us or made; and

Moffie told us the story of the accident in Cape Town, how the car crashed into the telephone box, and how he had gone rushing to help, and just when he got there the door of the car opened and a woman fell backwards into his arms. It nearly knocked him over, but he was able to hold her, and let her gently to the ground. And all the time the light was going off and on in the telephone box. And just when the light went on, he saw it was a Malay woman that he had in his arms, full of jewels and rings and blood. And he could not hold her any more; he let her go in horror, not even gently, he said, and even though a crowd was there. And without a word he pushed through the crowd and went on his way. For the touch of such a person was abhorrent to him, he said, and he did not think it was learned; he thought it was deep down in him, a part of his very nature. And many Afrikaners are the same.

Why Moffie's story should come back to me then I do not know, for I cannot remember that I had ever thought of it all these eleven years. But it came back to me now, and I thought of him, and of all those like him, with a deep envy, and a longing too, that I could have been like that myself.

How we laughed at Moffie's story, partly because of the way he told it, and partly, I suppose, because we were laughing at ourselves. I do not think we were laughing at the Malay woman, nor at the way he let her fall to the ground. And I suppose there was some shame in it too. But I would take the shame, and I would be like that myself, if I could; for to have such horror is to be safe. Therefore I envied him.

50

A

It was in sultry summer weather, and towards evening all of us boys and girls went out for a ramble on the plain, and were about a quarter of a mile from home when a blackness appeared in the south-west, and began to cover the sky in that quarter so rapidly that, taking alarm, we started homeward as fast as we could run. But the stupendous slaty-black darkness, mixed with yellow clouds of dust, gained on us, and before we got to the gate the terrified screams of wild birds reached our ears, and glancing back we saw multitudes of gulls and plover flying madly before the storm, trying to keep ahead of it. Then a swarm of big dragon-flies came like a cloud over us, and was gone in an instant, and just as we reached the gate the first big drops splashed down in the form of liquid mud. We had hardly got indoors before the tempest broke in its full fury, a blackness as of night, a blended uproar of thunder and wind, blinding flashes of lightning, and torrents of rain. Then as the first thick darkness began to pass away, we saw that the air was white with falling hail-stones of an extraordinary size and appearance. They were as big as fowls' eggs, but not egg-shaped: they were flat, and about half an inch thick, and being white, looked like little blocks or bricklets made of compressed snow. The hail continued falling until the earth was white with them, and in spite of their great size they were driven by the furious wind into drifts two or three feet deep against the walls of the buildings.

B

The wind was by now more than redoubled. The shutters were bulging as if tired elephants were leaning against them, and Father was trying to tie the fastening with a handkerchief. But to push against this wind was like pushing against rock. The handkerchief, shutters, everything burst; the rain poured in like the sea into a sinking ship, the wind occupied the room, snatching pictures from the wall, sweeping the room bare. Through the gaping frames the lightning-lit scene without was visible. The creepers, which before had looked like cobwebs, now streamed up into the sky like new-combed hair. Bushes were lying flat, laid back on the ground as close as a rabbit lays back his ears. Branches were leaping about loose in the sky. The negro huts were clean gone, and the negroes crawling on their stomachs across the compound to gain the shelter of the house. The bouncing rain seemed to cover the ground with a white smoke, a sort of sea in which the blacks wallowed like porpoises. One nigger-boy began to roll away; his mother, forgetting caution, rose to her feet: and immediately the fat old beldam was blown clean away, bowling across fields and hedgerows like someone in a funny fairy story, till she fetched up against a wall and was pinned there, unable to move. But the others managed to reach the house, and soon could be heard in the cellar underneath.

Moreover the very floor began to ripple, as a loose carpet will ripple on a gusty day: in opening the cellar door the blacks had let the wind in, and now for some time they could not shut it again. The wind, to push against, was more like a solid block than a current of air.

51

A   *Power*

Power, farmer? It was always yours.
Not the new physics' terrible threat
To the world's axle, nor the mind's subtler
Manipulation of our debt

To nature; but an old gift
For weathering the slow recoil
Of empires with a tree's patience,
Rooted in the dark soil.

B

Only a man harrowing clods
    In a slow silent walk
With an old horse that stumbles and nods
    Half asleep as they stalk.

Only thin smoke without flame
    From the heaps of couch-grass;
Yet this will go onward the same
    Though Dynasties pass.

Yonder a maid and her wight
    Come whispering by:
War's annals will cloud into night
    Ere their story die.

52

[Conrade and Borachio have been arrested by the watchmen. Constable Dogberry has been deputed to question them.]

Dogberry. Is our whole dissembly appear'd?

Verges. O, a stool and a cushion for the sexton!

Sexton. Which be the malefactors?

Dogb. Marry, that am I and my partner.

Verg. Nay, that's certain; we have the exhibition to examine.

Sext. But which are the offenders that are to be examin'd? Let them come before Master Constable.

Dogb. Yea, marry, let them come before me. What is your name, friend?

Bora. Borachio.

Dogb. Pray write down Borachio. Yours, sirrah?

Con. I am a gentleman, sir, and my name is Conrade.

Dogb. Write down Master Gentleman Conrade. Masters, do you serve God?

Con. ⎫
Bora. ⎭ Yea, sir, we hope.

Dogb. Write down that they hope they serve God; and write God first; for God defend but God should go before such villains! Masters, it is proved already that you are little better than false knaves, and it will go near to be thought so shortly. How answer you for yourselves?

Con. Marry, sir, we say we are none.

Dogb. A marvellous witty fellow, I assure you; but I will go about with him. Come you hither, sirrah; a word in your ear; sir, I say to you it is thought you are false knaves.

Bora. Sir, I say to you we are none.

Dogb. Well, stand aside. Fore God, they are both in a tale. Have you writ down that they are none?

Sext. Master Constable, you go not the way to examine; you must call forth the watch that are their accusers.

Dogb. Yea, marry, that's the eftest way. Let the watch come forth. Masters, I charge you in the Prince's name, accuse these men.

1 Watch. This man said, sir, that Don John, the Prince's brother, was a villain.

Dogb. Write down Prince John a villain. Why, this is flat perjury, to call a prince's brother villain.

Bora. Master Constable –

Dogb. Pray thee, fellow, peace; I do not like thy look, I promise thee.

Sext. What heard you him say else?

2 Watch. Marry, that he had received a thousand ducats of Don John for accusing the Lady Hero wrongfully.

Dogb. Flat burglary as ever was committed.

Verg. Yea, by mass, that it is.

Sext. What else, fellow?

1 Watch. And that Count Claudio did mean, upon his words, to disgrace Hero before the whole assembly, and not marry her.

Dogb. O villain! thou wilt be condemn'd into everlasting redemption for this.

53

London. Michaelmas Term lately over, and the Lord Chancellor sitting in Lincoln's Inn Hall. Implacable November weather. As much mud in the streets as if the waters had but newly retired from the face of the earth, and it would not be wonderful to meet a Megalosaurus, forty feet long or so, waddling like an elephantine lizard up Holborn Hill. Smoke lowering down from chimney-pots, making a soft black drizzle, with flakes of soot in it as big as fullgrown snowflakes – gone into mourning, one might imagine, for the death of the sun. Dogs, undistinguishable in mire. Horses, scarcely better; splashed to their very blinkers. Foot-passengers jostling one another's umbrellas, in a general infection of ill-temper, and losing their foot-hold at street-corners, where tens of thousands of other foot-passengers have been slipping and sliding since the day broke (if the day ever broke), adding new deposits to the crust upon crust of mud, sticking at those points tenaciously to the pavement, and accumulating at compound interest.

Fog everywhere. Fog up the river, where it flows among green aits and meadows; fog down the river, where it rolls defiled among the tiers of shipping, and the waterside pollutions of a great (and dirty) city. Fog on the Essex marshes, fog on the Kentish heights. Fog creeping into the cabooses of collier-brigs; fog lying out on the yards and hovering in the rigging of great ships; fog drooping on the gunwales of barges and small boats. Fog in the eyes and throats of ancient Greenwich pensioners, wheezing by the firesides of their wards; fog in the stem and bowl of the afternoon pipe of the wrathful skipper, down in his close cabin; fog cruelly pinching the toes and fingers of his shivering little prentice boy on deck. Chance people on the bridges peeping over the parapets into a nether sky of fog, with fog all around them, as if they were up in a balloon, and hanging in the misty clouds.

54

A   *Ex-Basketball Player*

Pearl Avenue runs past the high school lot,
Bends with the trolley tracks, and stops, cut off
Before it has a chance to go two blocks,
At Colonel McComsky Plaza. Berth's Garage
Is on the corner facing west, and there,
Most days, you'll find Flick Webb, who helps Berth out.

Flick stands tall among the idiot pumps –
Five on a side, the old bubble-head style,
Their rubber elbows hanging loose and low.
One's nostrils are two S's, and his eyes
An E and O. And one is squat, without
A head at all – more of a football type.

Once, Flick played for the high school team, the Wizards.
He was good: in fact, the best. In '46,
He bucketed three hundred ninety points,
A county record still. The ball loved Flick.
I saw him rack up thirty-eight or forty
In one home game. His hands were like wild birds.

He never learned a trade; he just sells gas,
Checks oil, and changes flats. Once in a while,
As a gag, he dribbles an inner tube,
But most of us remember anyway.
His hands are fine and nervous on the lug wrench.
It makes no difference to the lug wrench, though.

Off work, he hangs round Mae's Luncheonette.
Grease-grey and kind of coiled, he plays pinball,
Sips lemon cokes, and smokes those thin cigars;
Flick seldom speaks to Mae, just sits and nods
Beyond her face towards bright applauding tiers
Of Necco Wafers, Nibs, and Juju Beads.

B
Rugby League Game

Sport is absurd, and sad.
Those grown men, just look,
In those dreary long blue shorts,
Those ringed stockings, Edwardian,
Balding pates, and huge
Fat knees that ought to be heroes'.

Grappling, hooking, gallantly tackling –
Is all this courage really necessary? –
Taking their good clean fun
So solemnly, they run each other down
With earnest keenness, for the honour of
Virility, the cap, the county side.

Like great boys they roll each other
In the mud of public Saturdays,
Groping their blind way back
To noble youth, away from the bank,
The wife, the pram, the spin drier,
Back to the spartan freedom of the field.

Back, back to the days when boys
Were men, still hopeful, and untamed.

That was then: a gay
And golden age ago.
Now, in vain, domesticated,
Men try to be boys again.

55

A   *The Grave*

For thee was a house built
Ere thou was born,
For thee was a mould meant
Ere thou of mother camest.
But it is not made ready,
Nor is its depth measured,
Nor is it seen
How long it shall be.
Now I bring thee
Where thou shalt be;
Now I shall measure thee,
And the mould afterwards.

Thy house is not
Highly timbered,
It is unhigh and low;
When thou art therein,
The heel-ways are low,
The sideways unhigh.
The roof is built
Thy breast full nigh,
So thou shalt in mould
Dwell full cold,
Dimly and dark.

Doorless is that house,
And dark it is within;
There thou art fast detained,
And Death hath the key.

Loathsome is that earth-house,
And grim within to dwell.
There thou shalt dwell,
And worms shall divide thee.

Thus thou art laid,
And leavest thy friends;
Thou hast no friend,
Who will come to thee,
Who will ever see
How that house pleaseth thee;
Who will ever open
The door for thee
And descend after thee,
For soon thou art loathsome
And hateful to see.

B

Because I could not stop for Death
He kindly stopped for me.
The carriage held but just ourselves
And immortality.

We slowly drove. He knew no haste,
And I had put away
My labour and my leisure too
For his civility.

We passed the school where children strove
At recess in the ring.
We passed the fields of gazing grain;
We passed the setting sun –

Or rather, he passed us.
The dews drew quivering and chill,
For only gossamer my gown,
My tippet only tulle.

We passed before a house that seemed
A swelling of the ground.

The roof was scarcely visible,
The cornice in the ground.

Since then 'tis centuries, and yet
Feels shorter than the day
I first surmised the horses' heads
Were toward Eternity.

56

A

[As Antony enters Cleopatra's audience chamber he sees Thyreus, a messenger from Octavius, kissing Cleopatra's hand]

Antony.   Favours, by Jove that thunders!
What art thou, fellow?
Thyreus.   One that but performs
The bidding of the fullest man, and worthiest
To have command obey'd.
Enobarbus (aside).   You will be whipt.
Antony.   Approach there – Ah, you kite! – Now, gods and devils!
Authority melts from me. Of late, when I cried 'Ho!'
Like boys unto a muss, kings would start forth
And cry 'Your will?' Have you no ears?
I am Antony yet. Take hence this Jack and whip him.
. . . .
You were half blasted ere I knew you. Ha!
Have I my pillow left unpress'd in Rome,
Forborne the getting of a lawful race,
And by a gem of women, to be abus'd
By one that looks on feeders?
Cleopatra.   Good my Lord –
Antony.   You have been a boggler ever.
But when we in our viciousness grow hard –
O misery on't! – the wise gods seel our eyes,
In our own filth drop our clear judgements, make us
Adore our errors, laugh at's while we strut
To our confusion.
Cleopatra.   O, is't come to this?

Antony.   I found you as a morsel cold upon
Dead Caesar's trencher. Nay, you were a fragment
Of Cneius Pompey's, besides what hotter hours,
Unregister'd in vulgar fame, you have
Luxuriously pick'd out; for I am sure,
Though you can guess what temperance should be,
You know not what it is.

Cleopatra.   Wherefore is this?

Antony.   To let a fellow that will take rewards,
And say 'God quit you!' be familiar with
My playfellow, your hand, this kingly seal
And plighter of high hearts! . . .
        . . . .

Cleopatra.   Have you done yet?

Antony.   Alack, our terrene moon
Is now eclips'd and it portends alone
The fall of Antony.

Cleopatra.   I must stay his time.

Antony.   To flatter Caesar, would you mingle eyes
With one that ties his points?

Cleopatra.   Not know me yet?

Antony.   Cold-hearted toward me?

Cleopatra.   Ah, dear, if I be so,
From my cold heart let Heaven engender hail,
And poison it in the source, and the first stone
Drop in my neck; as it determines, so
Dissolve my life! The next Caesarion smite!
Till by degrees the memory of my womb,
Together with my brave Egyptians all,
By the discandying of this pelleted storm,
Lie graveless, till the flies and gnats of Nile
Have buried them for prey.

Antony.   I am satisfied.

B

[Julius Caesar, the Roman Commander, enters the king's council chamber at Alexandria to request money – Ptolemy, the king, a boy of ten, is surrounded by courtiers – Cleopatra is his sister.]

Pothinus (aghast). Forty million sesterces! Impossible. There is not so much money in the King's treasury.

Caesar (encouragingly). Only sixteen hundred talents, Pothinus. Why count it in sesterces? A sestertius is only worth a loaf of bread.

Pothinus. And a talent is worth a racehorse. I say it is impossible. We have been at strife here, because the King's sister Cleopatra falsely claims his throne. The King's taxes have not been collected for a whole year.

Caesar. Yes they have, Pothinus. My officers have been collecting them all the morning. (*Renewed whisper and sensation, not without some stifled laughter, among the courtiers.*)

Rufio (bluntly). You must pay, Pothinus. Why waste words? You are getting off cheaply enough.

Pothinus (bitterly). Is it possible that Caesar, the conqueror of the world, has time to occupy himself with such a trifle as our taxes?

Caesar. My friend, taxes are the chief business of a conqueror of the world.

Pothinus. Then take warning, Caesar. This day, the treasures of the temples and the gold of the King's treasury shall be sent to the mint to be melted down for our ransom in the sight of the people. They shall see us sitting under bare walls and drinking from wooden cups. And their wrath be on your head, Caesar, if you force us to this sacrilege!

Caesar. Do not fear, Pothinus: the people know how well wine tastes in wooden cups. In return for your bounty, I will settle this dispute about the throne for you, if you will. What say you?

Pothinus. If I say no, will that hinder you?

Rufio (defiantly). No.

Caesar. You say the matter has been at issue for a year, Pothinus. May I have ten minutes at it?

Pothinus. You will do your pleasure, doubtless.

Caesar. Good! But first, let us have Cleopatra here.

Theodotus. She is not in Alexandria: she is fled into Syria.

Caesar. I think not. (*to Rufio*) Call Totateeta.

Rufio (calling). Ho there, Teetatota.

(*Ftatateeta enters the loggia, and stands arrogantly at the top of the steps.*)

Ftat. Who pronounces the name of Ftatateeta, the Queen's chief nurse?

Caesar. Nobody can pronounce it, Tota, except yourself. Where is your mistress?

(*Cleopatra, who is hiding behind Ftatateeta, peeps out at them, laughing. Caesar rises.*)

Caesar. Will the Queen favour us with her presence for a moment?

Cleopatra (*pushing Ftatateeta aside and standing haughtily on the steps*). Am I to behave like a Queen?

Caesar. Yes.

(*Cleopatra immediately comes down to the chair of state; seizes Ptolemy; drags him out of his seat; then takes his place in the chair. Ftatateeta seats herself on the step of the loggia, and sits there, watching the scene with sibylline intensity.*)

Ptolemy (*mortified, and struggling with his tears*). Caesar: this is how she treats me always. If I am a king why is she allowed to take everything from me?

Cleopatra. You are not to be King, you little cry-baby. You are to be eaten by the Romans.

Caesar (*touched by Ptolemy's distress*). Come here, my boy, and stand by me.

(*Ptolemy goes over to Caesar, who, resuming his seat on the tripod, takes the boy's hand to encourage him. Cleopatra, furiously jealous, rises and glares at them.*)

Cleopatra (*with flaming cheeks*). Take your throne: I don't want it. (*She flings away from the chair, and approaches Ptolemy, who shrinks from her.*) Go this instant and sit down in your place.

Caesar. Go, Ptolemy. Always take a throne when it is offered to you.

Rufio. I hope you will have the good sense to follow your own advice when we return to Rome, Caesar.

57

[from *A Modest Proposal* for preventing the children of poor people in Ireland from being a burden to their parents or country, and for making them beneficial to the public. 1729.]

I have been assured by a very knowing American of my acquaintance in London, that a young healthy child well nursed is at a year old a most delicious, nourishing, and wholesome food, whether stewed, roasted, baked or boiled; and I make no doubt that it will equally serve in a fricassee or a ragout.

I do therefore humbly offer it to public consideration that of the 120,000 children already computed, 20,000 may be reserved for breed . . . [and] that the remaining 100,000 may at a year old, be offered in sale to the persons of quality and fortune through the kingdom . . . A child will make two dishes at an entertainment for friends; and when the family dines alone, the fore or hind quarter will make a reasonable dish, and seasoned with a little pepper or salt will be very good boiled on the fourth day, especially in winter . . .

I grant this food will be somewhat dear, and therefore very proper for landlords, who, as they have already devoured most of the parents, seem to have the best title to the children.

Infant's flesh will be in season throughout the year . . . I believe no gentleman would repine to give 10s. for the carcass of a good fat child, which as I have said will make four dishes of excellent nutritive meat . . . Thus the squire will learn to be a good landlord, and grow popular among his tenants; the mother will have 8s. net profit, and be fit for work till she produces another child.

Those who are more thrifty (as I must confess the times require) may flay the carcass; the skin of which artificially dressed will make admirable gloves for ladies, and summer boots for fine gentlemen . . .

A very worthy person . . . was lately pleased in discoursing on this matter to offer a refinement on my scheme. He . . . conceived that the want of venison might be well supplied by the bodies of young lads and maidens, not exceeding 14 years of age nor under 12. . . . But with due deference to so excellent a friend and so deserving a patriot, I cannot be altogether in his sentiments; for as to the males, my American acquaintance assured me, from frequent experience, that their flesh was generally tough and lean, like that of our schoolboys by continual exercise, and their taste disagreeable; and to fatten them would not answer the charge. Then as to the females, it would I think with humble submission be a loss to the public, because they soon would become breeders themselves; and besides, it is not improbable that some scrupulous people might be apt to censure such a practice (although indeed very unjustly), as a little bordering upon cruelty; which, I confess has always been with me the strongest objection against any project, how well soever intended . . .

I profess, in the sincerity of my heart, that I have not the least personal interest in endeavouring to promote this necessary work, having no other motive than the public good of my country, by advancing our trade, providing for infants, relieving the poor, and giving some pleasure to the rich. I have no children by which I can propose to get a single penny; the youngest being nine years old, and my wife past child-bearing.

Some suggestions for written work based on the passages
(numbers refer to the 57 items in Chapter Four).

1. Compare the aims of the three writers, showing how they affect their manner of presenting the events described.

2. *Either* (a) In each piece a song is sung. Compare your impressions of the two songs. For which writer is the song more important? What feeling does each writer show?
Or (b) Use these two pieces of writing to illustrate an essay or discussion on sentimentality in literature.

3. Each poem is concerned with the poet's craft. What assumptions does each poet make about his craft? Which seems the more direct in its impact on the reader? (No. 28 provides an additional example.)

4. The situations portrayed are closely similar. Comment in detail on the differences in presentation, *or* compare the behaviour of Jack and Christy.

7. What does this extract from a novel tell us about the relationships between these parents and their children? What confidence would you place in Captain Marpole? Decide on the writer's intention here by assessing his tone.

9. Compare the rhythm and rhyme-schemes, drawing conclusions about the poet's theme and intentions. (Poem B is discussed in Chapter Two. See also example no. IV in Chapter Three.)

11. In what ways does the style of each poem indicate the level at which it is to be read? Which demands more from the reader?

13. Discuss and illustrate this writer's descriptive skill in this excerpt from a long narrative poem.

14. Assess what audience is being addressed in this passage, explaining what evidence leads you to your conclusion. (The passage can be studied together with no. V in Chapter Three.)

15. Compare the handling of words in these two short fictional excerpts.

17. Examine the style of these extracts and say what different effects the two novelists are aiming at, and how successfully they achieve them.

19. What is each poet's attitude towards conservation? How successfully does each state his case?

23. Extracts A and B are from novels, C from a book on architecture. How do the language employed and the selection of features commented on relate to the writers' purposes?

26. Write about the way Stephen's personality is illuminated here.

27. What does the conversation reveal about each character, and about their relations with each other?

28. Examine closely the structure, rhyme-scheme and imagery, and relate them to the poet's theme. (This poem can also be used with the poems in no. 3.)

29. Compare the three attitudes to Fame and old age. Which appeals to you most? (The poems in no. 9 can be studied with these.)

30. (a) What assumptions does the writer make about his audience?
(b) Discuss the likely reasons for the cuts in the public reading version.

31. What comment is the second poet making about the first poem, or about its subject-matter?

33. Describe your impression of the nature of the relationship between Willie and Rose. What, in the dialogue, conveys that impression?

34. How seriously are we expected to take this episode? Compare the author's with the speaker's attitude to the events described.

38. (a) What does this reveal of the man's feelings?
(b) Compare the method of writing with no. 49B, which is on a similar theme, but from a novel.

40. (a) Both these pieces of writing describe paintings. Which brings out more clearly the quality of the painting being described?
(b) Compare the feeling shown by the writers.

43. What is this dialogue about?

45. Compare the style of these two comments on the art of translation. Do the writers agree at all?

46. (a) How are we made aware of Voss's feelings on this occasion?
(b) What differences do you find between the novelist's technique here and the dramatist's in no. 56B?

47. Compare the approach of the poet to his subject with no. 24.

48. Both of these short lyrics have been successfully set to music.

SOME SUGGESTIONS FOR WRITTEN WORK

What qualities of the language – and perhaps of the theme as well – make them suitable for this?

49. *Either* (a) Use both these passages to demonstrate the novelist's need to present his story in a social setting; *Or*
(b) What features of the social settings are revealed here? How do they differ?

50. One of the passages comes from a novel, the other from an autobiography. Decide which is which, supporting your choice with reference to the styles.

52. What makes this scene funny?

53. *Either* (a) What is the novelist's main purpose here? How successfully does he achieve it? *Or*
(b) Compare the descriptive method here with that in no. I, Chapter Three.

56. Compare the writers' attitudes to their subject-matter, as revealed by their language.

57. What is this writer's aim? Do you think the piece from which this extract is taken would be successful in achieving it? Consider carefully the tone of the writing.

Chapter 3: I John Updike *Rabbit Run*; II Ben Jonson *Volpone*; III T. S. Eliot; IV W. B. Yeats; V A Sir James Jeans, V B J. L. Russell.

Chapter 4:

1. Thomas Hardy *A Pair of Blue Eyes*; Celia Fiennes *Journeys*; Damart Ltd.
2. Charles Reade *The Cloister and the Hearth*; D. H. Lawrence
3. Arthur O'Shaughnessy; Basil Bunting
4. Richard Brinsley Sheridan *The Rivals*; J. M. Synge *Playboy of the Western World*
5. John Ormond; Seamus Heaney
6. Ben Jonson; anon. *Everyman*
7. Richard Hughes *A High Wind in Jamaica*
8. Thomas Dekker *The Shoemakers' Holiday*
9. W. B. Yeats; Thomas Hardy
10. Anthony Conran
11. William Shakespeare; G. Mason
12. William Shakespeare *The Merchant of Venice*
13. William Shakespeare *Venus and Adonis*
14. Fred Hoyle *The Nature of the Universe*
15. Katherine Mansfield *Bliss*; James Joyce *Ulysses*
16. Elizabeth Bishop
17. Walter Macken *Rain on the Wind*; William Golding *Pincher Martin*
18. Samuel Plimsoll *Our Seamen* (1873); Edmund Burke
19. Gerard Manley Hopkins; R. S. Thomas
20. John Webster *The Duchess of Malfi*
21. Philip Larkin
22. William Shakespeare *Cymbeline*
23. Jane Austen *Pride and Prejudice*; F. Scott Fitzgerald *The Great Gatsby*; Nicholas Pevsner *The Buildings of England: Shropshire*
24. Wilfred Owen
25. Robert Herrick; William Blake
26. James Joyce *A Portrait of the Artist as a Young Man*
27. Arthur Miller *A View from the Bridge*
28. Dylan Thomas
29. Robert Graves; Alfred, Lord Tennyson; Matthew Arnold

Acknowledgements

Thanks are due to the following authors, or their representatives, and publishers for permission to reprint the following copyright items:

The Editor of *Agenda* for a quotation from 'Some Recent Paintings of David Jones' on p. 38 of Vol. 5, Nos 1–3.

Sir John Betjeman and John Murray, Publishers, Ltd, for 'Executive' from *A Nip in the Air*.

Elizabeth Bishop, Farrar, Straus & Giroux, Inc. and Chatto & Windus Ltd for 'The Filling Station' from *The Complete Poems*.

Basil Bunting and Oxford University Press for 'What the Chairman told Tom' from *Collected Poems* © Basil Bunting 1978.

Charles Causley and the Macmillan Co. for 'Infant Song' from *Collected Poems*.

Anthony Conran and Christopher Davies, Publishers, Ltd for 'Factory Worker' from *Spirit Level*.

Damart Thermawear Ltd for part of an advertisement for Damart Thermawear.

Faber & Faber Ltd for lines from T. S. Eliot's *The Family Reunion*.

D. J. Enright and Chatto & Windus Ltd for 'A Polished Performance' from *Selected Poems*.

King's College, Cambridge and the Society of Authors on behalf of the E. M. Forster Estate, also Sidgwick & Jackson, for an extract from *The Celestial Omnibus*.

Athol Fugard and Oxford University Press for an extract from *Statements After an Arrest Under the Immorality Act*.

William Golding and Faber & Faber Ltd for an extract from *Pincher Martin*.

Grants of St James's for part of an advertisement for Goldener Oktober.

Robert Graves and Cassell & Co. for 'Troublesome Fame' from *The Collected Poems*.

D. W. Harding and Cambridge University Press for a passage from *Words into Rhythm*.

Seamus Heaney and Faber & Faber Ltd for 'Thatcher' from *Door into the Dark*.

Geoffrey Hill and André Deutsch Ltd for fourteen lines from *Mercian Hymns*.

ACKNOWLEDGEMENTS

Sir Fred Hoyle and Basil Blackwell, Publisher, for an extract from *The Nature of the Universe*.

Chatto & Windus Ltd for two extracts from Richard Hughes' *A High Wind in Jamaica*.

Cambridge University Press for an extract from Sir James Jeans' *The Mysterious Universe*.

The Bodley Head Ltd for an extract from James Joyce's *Ulysses*.

Jonathan Cape Ltd for an extract from James Joyce's *A Portrait of the Artist as a Young Man*.

Richard Kell and Chatto & Windus Ltd for 'Poet on the Brink' from *Control Tower*.

James Kirkup for 'Rugby League Game'.

Philip Larkin and Faber & Faber Ltd for 'Mr Bleaney' from *The Whitsun Weddings*.

The Estate of the late Mrs Frieda Lawrence Ravagli, Laurence Pollinger Ltd and William Heinemann Ltd for 'Piano' from the *Complete Poems of D. H. Lawrence* and for an extract from *Lady Chatterley's Lover*.

Norman MacCaig and The Hogarth Press Ltd for 'July Evening' from *A Round of Applause*.

Walter Macken and the Macmillan Co. for an extract from *Rain on the Wind*.

Thomas McGrath and the Swallow Press Inc. for 'A Coalfire in Winter' from *Movie at the End of the World*.

James Michie for 'At Any Rate' from *Possible Laughter*.

Arthur Miller and Secker & Warburg Ltd for an excerpt from *A View from the Bridge*, included in *Collected Plays* © Arthur Miller 1955, 1957.

John Ormond and Oxford University Press for 'The Piano Tuner' from *Definition of a Waterfall* (copyright 1973).

Alan Paton and Jonathan Cape Ltd for an extract from *Too Late the Phalarope*.

Nikolaus Pevsner and Penguin Books Ltd for an extract from *Shropshire* (The Buildings of England) © Nikolaus Pevsner 1958.

Harold Pinter and Eyre Methuen Ltd for an extract from *The Caretaker*.

Faber & Faber Ltd for twelve lines from 'The Seafarer' from *Selected Poems of Ezra Pound*.

Miss F. F. Quiller-Couch for 'The Least of These' by Sir Arthur Quiller-Couch.

READING AND DISCRIMINATION

abstraction: the considering of qualities apart from concrete examples: 'displaced persons' for 'refugees'.

accent: a stressed syllable: 'con′sequence', 'misan′thropist'.

alliteration: the repetition of a consonant at the beginning of successive words: 'the dance of death'.

allusion: the reference to a word or phrase from literature or history, for the sake of its associations.

anticlimax: the descent from the sublime to the ridiculous.

antithesis: the contrasting of ideas by juxtaposing words of opposite or apparently opposite meaning: 'Christ the tiger'.

archaism: the use of an old-fashioned word or construction.

assonance: the repetition of identical or similar vowel sounds: 'time out of mind', 'lisp of leaves and ripple of rain'.

bathos: see *anticlimax*.

blank verse: ten-syllabled lines without rhyme.

caesura: the natural break in a line of verse.

cliché: a hackneyed expression.

colloquial: in the style of conversation.

conceit: a figure of speech involving a comparison, usually far-fetched.

concrete: in the form of actual examples; giving particular instances.

connote: (of words) suggesting more than the primary meaning, e.g. 'autumn' denotes the season after summer, but according to the context it connotes one or more of: fruitfulness, harvesting, maturity, the approach to old age.

couplet: two successive lines of rhyming verse.

denote: to point to, to signify, to distinguish, cf. *connote*.

diction: the choice of words and phrases, the kind of vocabulary that characterises a piece of writing.

doggerel: uncouth or clumsy verse.

elegy: a poem on a death, hence any serious meditative verse.

emotive: charged with feeling, stirring up feeling.

end-stopped: describes a line of verse in which the sense ends naturally with the line ending.

enjambement: a feature of verse in which the sense over-runs the line ending. E.g. Wordsworth's 'Upon Westminster Bridge'.

READING AND DISCRIMINATION

euphony: pleasant sound, a musical quality. Cf. 'cacophony'.

figurative language: uses such means as metaphor to convey more meaning than literal statement.

figure of speech: a departure from literal or scientific meaning, such as 'metaphor', 'personification', 'simile', etc.

foot: a unit of metrical verse.

free verse: a way of writing poetry without rhyme or metre.

heroic couplet: two rhymed iambic pentameters.

imagery: the use of mental pictures to suggest what can be seen, heard, felt, tasted or sensed; every kind of comparison.

irony: a figure of speech in which the words mean the opposite of what is outwardly said. Its success depends on the reader's recognition of the author's intention.

jargon: originally the special language of particular groups, now often applied to longwinded officialese.

lyric: formerly a song, now almost any short non-narrative poem.

magniloquent: lofty in expression.

meaning: can be seen to include four elements: intention, the writer's aim; the sense, the literal meaning; feeling, the writer's emotional involvement in his subject; and tone, the writer's attitude to his audience.

metaphor: the figure of speech whereby one thing or experience is seen in terms of another, as in these examples from daily speech: 'loud colours', 'sparkling wit', 'dark hints', 'a warm welcome'. Cf. 'simile', in which a direct comparison is introduced by 'like' or 'as'.

metre: a verse pattern conforming to a certain arrangement of stressed syllables.

movement: the way verse goes – brisk, hesitant, smooth, jerky, feeble, etc.

onomatopoeia: the imitation of sounds by words – 'click', 'rattle', 'bang', 'buzz', 'the murmur of innumerable bees'.

paradox: an apparently self-contradictory statement.

periphrasis: a roundabout way of putting things; 'humble instrument of honest toil' for 'spade'.

personification: the attribution of life to an abstract quality etc.: 'old father time'.

poetic diction: words and expression used in poetry but not in everyday usage. E.g. much eighteenth-century verse.

refrain: the regular repetition of words or phrases in poetry, originally an opportunity for listeners to join in. E.g. many ballads and George Herbert's 'Virtue'.

rhyme: the identity of sound in the final syllables of words, normally occurring at the ends of verse lines. In oral poetry a memorising device and a means of holding the audience's attention. Wilfred Owen and others used half-rhymes to create moods of uncertainty, doubt, wrongness.

rhythm: (i) a recognised pattern in the occurrence of stresses and pauses, or (ii) the way in which a poem, e.g. in free verse, is read to bring out the full meaning apprehended by a person who has fully responded to it.

sentimentality: an excessive or inappropriate emotional response.

sincerity: the force with which an artist of any kind experiences the sensation, mood and so on that he is sharing with others. Negatively (in I. A. Richards' words): 'the absence of any apparent attempt on the part of the artist to work effects upon the reader which do not work for himself'.

stanza: a group of lines of verse, often conforming to a metrical scheme.

stock response: a stereotyped reaction to literature, preventing a genuine responsiveness.

symbols: in Blake's poem

> The sword sung on the barren heath,
> The sickle in the fruitful field:
> The sword he sung a song of death,
> But could not make the sickle yield

the sword and the sickle are symbols, standing for war and agriculture respectively.

Set, printed and bound in Great Britain by
Cox & Wyman Ltd., London, Fakenham and Reading